T0150788

THE MAGIC ORACLE BOOK

THE MAGIC ORACLE BOOK

Ask Any Question and Discover Your Fate

CERRIDWEN GREENLEAF

CORAL GABLES

For permission requests, please contact the publisher at:
Mango Publishing Group
2850 S Douglas Road, 2nd Floor
Coral Gables, FL 33134 USA
info@mango.bz

For special orders, quantity sales, course adoptions and corporate sales, please
email the publisher at sales@mango.bz. For trade and wholesale sales, please
contact Ingram Publisher Services at customer.service@ingramcontent.com or
+1.800.509.4887.

The Magic Oracle Book: Ask Any Question and Discover Your Fate

Library of Congress Cataloging-in-Publication number: 2019948831
ISBN: (print) 978-1-64250-182-7, (ebook) 978-1-64250-183-4
BISAC category code ########

Printed in the United States of America

Dedicated to the loving memory of Roberto Kent Leffler

TABLE OF CONTENTS

INTRODUCTION: YOUR DIVINATION STATION

Becoming conscious of the possibilities is the first step in *The Magic Oracle Book*. Daily spiritual practices and seasonal rituals create a life filled with blessings. One ancient ritual I discovered early on was bibliomancy, a form of divination developed when books were precious objects made of papyrus, vellum, or even rolled up leaves.

Even when I was girl, I used to love to open books at random and get my message for the day. I had no idea about this, but it turns out I was in accordance with a marvelous and quite ancient form of divination, that of bibliomancy. It is one of the simplest rituals you can do to connect with the divine in an instant and easy way. Bibliomancy is a simple ritual that I have incorporated into my daily life for inspiration "from the heavens." Simply open this book at random and let a word or phrase come to your attention. You thus become inspired in the true meaning of the word, which is simply to breathe in the power of the gods and goddesses. In this simple, direct, and powerful way, you will connect with the divine every time you dip into this oracular tome.

I have my own copy of this very book on my altar. Whenever I need it (and sometimes that is several times a day!), I will pick it up, take a deep breath, and speak my question aloud. Then, eyes closed for a moment, I pick a place on a page. You will be amazed at how helpful this practice is and how grounded you will feel afterward. Let this book become a touchstone for you and a light in dark times. Sometimes, all we need are the right words at the right time, and my hope for you is that *The Magic*

Oracle Book will bring a spark of magic into your life every single day.

May you be blessed on your journey,

CERRIDWEN

HOW TO USE
THE MAGIC ORACLE

The Magic Oracle is designed to be spontaneous and filled with poetry, just like life itself. While there are no hard and fast rules to consulting this book, we offer these guidelines to loosely follow. Are you a haiku person, or do you prefer free verse? Your own preference will guide you to the manner in which you use The Magic Oracle.

Set the book upon a flat surface; if no surface is available, you may hold the book in your open palms.

For questions of a more serious nature, candle light is recommended, and it is even more divine if this is the only light in the room. Fire light is also nice. The Magic Oracle is very personal. You decide what you will seek from it.

Close your eyes and concentrate on the question or quandary at hand. When you have taken the time to really focus on what you need to know, keeping your eyes closed, begin to flip the pages. Stop when you feel you have reached a place that will answer your imploring thoughts, and use your index finger to point to a place on the page. Open your eyes and read the passage nearest your finger. This is the gift that The Magic Oracle offers you.

To remain truly inspired, you may want to use that verse to start a free-write of your own. Or perhaps if you are in a group, the stanzas all fit together somehow? The Magic Oracle strives to pay tribute to the thousands of poignant stanzas that have changed our thinking. We invite you to join along.

THE MAGIC ORACLE

My faultless breast the furnace is, the fuel wounding thorns,

Love is the fire, and signs the smoke,

The ashes shame and scornes.

Robert Southwell, "The Burning Babe"

The life we begin with a scream

we end with a whisper.

Bucky Sinister, "The House that Punk Built"

In the meantime, if you demand on the one hand,

the raw material of poetry in

all its rawness and

that which is on the other hand

genuine, you are interested in poetry.

Marianne Moore, "Poetry"

The Lady is a humble thing

Made of death and water

The fashion is to dress it plain

And use the mind for border.

Elise Cowen, "The Lady Is a Humble Thing"

So sat I between the word truth

And the word fable

Took out my empty bowl

And spoon.

Charles Simic, "Pastoral"

I must go to the mountainsto hear

the sound and the sound.

Kijo Song, "Sound"

To drift with every passion till my soul

Is a stringed lute on which all winds can play,

Is it for this that I have given away

Mine ancient wisdom, and austere control?

Oscar Wilde, "Helas"

And graven with diamonds in letters plain

There is written, her fair neck round about,

Noli me Tangere, for Caesar's I am,

And wild for to hold, though I seem tame.

Sir Thomas Wyatt the Elder, "Whoso List to Hunt"

There is neither heaven nor earth,

Only snow

Falling incessantly.

Hashin, "The First Snow of the Year"

I cannot abide these malapert males,

Pirates of love who know no duty;

Yet love with a storm can take down their sales,

And they must strike to Admiral Beauty.

Sir William Davenant, "Plays and Masques"

That if gold ruste, what shal iren doo?

Geoffrey Chaucer, *The Canterbury Tales*

And cannot pleasures, while they last,

Be actual unless, when past,

They leave us shuddering and aghast,

With anguish smarting?

Lewis Carroll, "A Valentine"

Know you faire on what you look;

Divinest love lyes in this booke.

Richard Cranshaw, "The Temple of Sacred Poems"

O get thee wings!

Henry Vaughan, "The British Church"

Doing, a filthy pleasure is, and short;

And done, we straight repent us of the sport

Petronius Arbiter, "Doing, a filthy pleasure is, and short"

Wine comes in at the mouth

And love comes in at the eye.

William Butler Yeats, "A Drinking Song"

Rich men, trust not in wealth,

Gold cannot buy your health

Thomas Nashe, "Adieu, Farewell, Earth's Bliss"

Something sinister in the tone

Told me my secret must be known.

Robert Frost, "Bereft"

Come in the evening, or come in the morning;
Come when you're look'd for, or come without warning.

Thomas Osbourne Davis, "The Welcome"

THE ANSWER LIES WITHIN

Here at our sea-washed, sunset gates shall stand
A mighty woman with a torch, whose flame
Is the imprisoned lightning, and her name,
Mother of Exiles.

Emma Lazarus, "The New Colossus"

There are no people
To gape at them now,
For people are loath to
Peer in the dimness.

Padraic Colum, "Monkeys"

The least flower with a brimming cup may stand,
And share its dew-drop with another near.

Elizabeth Barrett Browning, "Work"

You did not come,

And marching Time drew on, and wore me numb.

Thomas Hardy, "A Broken Appointment"

The pulp so bitter, how shall taste the rind?

Francis Thompson, "The Hound of Heaven"

O drinke to thirst, and thirst to drinke that treasurer,

where the only danger is to keepe a measurer.

William Alabaster, "Sonnet 32"

This cynic smile is but a wile of guile

This costume chaste is

But good taste misplaced!

Martin Gordon, "Am I Alone?"

And in his mistress' flame, playing like a fly,

Turned to cinders by her eye?

Yes; and in death, as life, unblessed,

To have't expressed,

Even ashes of lovers find no rest.

Ben Jonson, "The Hourglass"

There is a channel between voice and presence,
where information flows.

In disciplined silence the channel opens;
with wandering talk, it closes.

Rumi, "Afghanistan"

How happy he, who free from care

The rage of courts, and noise of towns;

Contented breathes his native air,

In his own grounds.

Alexander Pope, "Ode on Solitude"

Velvet at the edge of the tongue,

at the edge of the brain, it was

velvet. At the edge of history.

Diane di Prima, "For Pigpen"

The tumult and the shouting dies;

The captains and the kings depart:

Still stands Thine ancient sacrifice,

An humble and a contrite heart.

Rudyard Kipling, "Recessional"

And the greatest gift

God can give is His own experience.

Meister Eckhart, "To See As God Sees"

THE ANSWER IS NO

Busy old fool, unruly Sun,

Why dost thou thus,

Through windows, and through curtains call on us?

John Donne, "The Sun Rising"

And if I should live to be

The last leaf upon the tree

In the spring,

Let them smile, as I do now,

At the old forsaken bough

Where I cling.

Oliver Wendell Holmes, "The Last Leaf"

Can there be any day but this,

Though many sunnes to shine endeavour?

We count three hundred, but we misse:

There is but one, and that one ever.

George Herbert, "Easter"

Not good for the land, not good for the sea

There's nothing biodegradable about it

But it does make one hell of an outfit.

Jessyka Stinston, "Tinsel Me Pretty"

That now are wild, and do not remember

That sometime they put themselves in danger

To take bread at my hand; and now they range,

Busily seeking with a continual change.

Sir Thomas Wyatt the Elder, "They Flee from Me"

Look
what happens to the scale
when love
holds
it.
It
stops
working.

Kabir, "It Stops Working"

Swore that two lives should be like one

As long as the sea-gull loved the sea,

As long as the sunflower sought the sun,—

It shall be, I said, for eternity

'Twixt you and me!

Oscar Wilde, "Her Voice"

But cease thy tears, bid ev'ry sigh depart,

And cast the load of anguish from thine heart:

From the cold shell of his great soul arise,

And look beyond, thou native of the skies.

Phillis Wheatley, "To a Lady on the Death of Her Husband"

Who sayes that fictions only and false hair

Become a verse? Is there in truth no beauty?

George Herbert, "Jordan (I)"

Yet haste the era, when the world shall know,

That such distinctions only dwell below;

The soul unfetter'd, to no sex confin'd,

Was for the abodes of cloudless day designed.

Judith Sargent Murray, "On the Equality of Sexes"

All we can touch, swallow, or say

Aids in our crossing to God

And helps unveil the soul.

Saint Theresa of Avila, "I Loved What I Could Love"

Man is a shop of ruses: a well truss'd pack,

Whose every parcel under-writes a law.

Lose not thyself, nor give thy humors way;

God gave them to thee under lock and key.

George Herbert, "The Church-Porch"

The church is put in fault;

The prelates been so haut,

They say, and look so high

As though they would fly

Above the starry sky.

John Skelton, "From Colin Clout"

BUT NOW, WITH NEW AND OPEN EYES,

I SEE BENEATH, AS IF I WERE

ABOVE THE SKIES.

THOMAS TRAHERNE, "THE THIRD CENTURY"

Without sound we live in.

Where we are, really, climbing

the sides of buildings to peer in like spiderman,
at windows not our own.

Diane di Prima, "My Lover's Eyes Are Nothing Like The Sun"

And coward Love, then, to the heart apace

Taketh his flight, where he doth lurk and 'plain,

His purpose lost, and dare not show his face.

**Henry Howard, Earl Of Surrey, "Love, That Doth Reign
and Live Within My Thought"**

Who calls me that

As I go further into emptiness

I find something greater emptied

Something greater than heaven emptied.

Seuk Hô, "Something Greater Than Heaven"

Rash is the man, when the black banners blow,

What weds wi' the Queen o' the Castle o' Crow.

Helen Adam, "The Queen O' Crow Castle"

Green Buddhas

On the fruit stand.

We eat the smile

And spit out the teeth.

Charles Simic, "Watermelons"

When reading all those thick books on the life of god,

It should be noted that they were all written by men.

Bob Kaufman, "Heavy Water Blues"

She cries loudly for us to come! We hear,

for the night's many tongues

carry her cry across the sea.

Sappho, "To Atthis"

IT IS CERTAIN

We who bear your creation seek re-creation.

Plant in your people a love and respect for your land.

Plant in your people a love and respect for your land.

Martin Palmer, "Listen to the Voices of Creation"

Life smooths us, rounds, perfects,

as does the river the stone,

and there is no place our Beloved is not flowing

though the current's force you may not always like.

Saint Theresa of Avila, "I Loved What I Could Love"

What? Not done complaining yet?

Anne Waldman, "A Phonecall from Frank O' Hara"

All the false notions of myself that once caused fear, pain,
have turned to ash as I neared God.

Hafiz, "Persia"

To goe to heaven, we make heaven come to us.

We spur, we rein the starres, and in their race

They're diversely content t'obey our pace.

John Donne, "The First Anniversary; An Anatomy of the World"

Light came from the east, bright signal of God, the sea
became still so that I might see the headlands, the windy
walls of the sea. Fate often saves an undoomed man when his
courage is good.

Beowulf, "The Feast at Herot"

But Oh! What Human Fortitude can be

Sufficient to Resist a Deity?

Aphra Behn, "A Congratulatory Poem"

Shall you have all or nothing

take half or pass by untouched?

Marge Piercy, "My Mother's Body"

Our passions help to lift us.

I loved what I could love until I held Him,

for then-all things-every world disappeared.

Saint Theresa of Avila, "Spain"

The shell must break before the bird can fly.

Alfred Lord Tennyson, "The Ancient Sage"

LOOK WITHIN

O kill kill kill kill kill

Those who advertise you out.

Charles Olson, "I, Maximus of Gloucester, to You"

And with a beck ye shall me call,

And if of one that burneth always

Ye have any pity at all,

Answer him fair with yea or nay.

Sir Thomas Wyatt the Elder, "Without Many Words"

They seem anxious to know

What holds up heaven nowadays.

James Merrill, "After Greece"

Like water in goblets of unbaked clay

I drip out slowly,

and dry.

My soul whirls. Dizzy. Let me

discover my home.

Lal Ded

God Damn you God damn me my misunderstanding of you.

Charles Olson, "Moonset, Gloucester, December 1, 1957, 1:58 a.m."

Alas! It is a fearful thing

To feel another's guilt!

Oscar Wilde, "The Ballad of Reading Gaol"

Even so you can see in full dawn

The ground there lifts

a foreign thing desertless in origin.

A.R. Ammons, "Apologia Pro Vita Sua"

Next, sip this weak wine

From the green glass flask,

with its stopper.

Robert Browning, "The Englishman in Italy"

A coin, a dot, the end of a sentence,

the end of the long improbable utterance

of the holy and human.

C.K. Williams, "The Modern"

We are resident inside the machinery,

a glimmering spread throughout the apparatus.

Jack Gilbert, "Kunstkammer"

You sing in my mind like wine. What you

did not dare in your life you dare in mine.

Marge Piercy, "My Mother's Body"

Crossed your bridge with your big word and your huge silence.

ruth weiss, "For Bobby Kaufman"

The teeming gulf—the sleepers and the shadows!

The past—the infinite greatness of the past!

For what is the present after all but a growth out of the past?

Walt Whitman, "Passage to India"

This piece of food cannot be eaten,

nor this bit of wisdom found by looking.

There is a secret core in everyone not

even Gabriel can know by trying to know.

Rumi

The worldy wisdome of the foolish man

Is like a sieve, that does, alone, retain

The grosser substance of the worthless brain.

Francis Quables, "Book 2, Emblem VII"

Thy lust and liking is from thee gone.

Thou blinkard blowboll, thou wakest too late.

John Skelton, "Lullay, Lullay, Like a Child"

These are the tranquillized Fifties
And I am forty. Ought I to regret my seedtime?

Robert Lowell. "Memories of West Street and Lepke"

The people I love the best jump into work head first
without dallying in the shallows
and swim off with sure strokes almost out of sight.

Marge Piercy, "To Be of Use"

you can be a good girl
and stop
telling everyone what you're doing
when you are abusing
drugs and men
and bodies
that look something like your own

perine parker, "denial"

Man is all symmetrie
Full of proportions, one limbe to another,
And all to all the world besides:
Each part may call the farthest, brother

George Herbert, "Man"

None thither mounts by the degree
Of knowledge, but humility.

Andrew Marvell, "A Dialogue, Between the Resolved Soul, and Created Pleasure"

To rack old Elements,
Or Dust;
and say
Sure here he must needs stay
Is not the way, nor Just.

Henry Vaughan, "The Search"

THIS IS
ALWAYS THE CASE.
WHEREVER I AM
I AM WHAT IS MISSING.

MARK STRAND, "KEEPING THINGS WHOLE"

No darkness then did overshade,
But all within was Pure and Bright,
No Guilt did Crush, nor fear invade
But all my Soul was full of Light.

Thomas Traherne, "Innocence"

The only war that matters

is the war against the imagination.

Diane di Prima, "Rant"

Suffering is what was born

Ignorance made me forlorn

Tearful truths I cannot scorn

Allen Ginsberg, "Don't Grow Old"

Dear philosophers, I get sad when I think.

Is it the same with you?

Charles Simic, "A Letter"

A spark of recognition and she

Mouths the words

Takes his hand

G. Thomas, "Warsaw"

This Planet will survive only if

All recognize a Common Mission.

Norbert Korte, "There's No Such Thing As an Ex-Catholic"

She cries loudly for us to come!

We hear, for the night's many tongues

carry her cry across the sea.

Sappho, "To Atthis"

tonight I am the only one who knows me

and I hallucinate.

eli coppola, "Who Am I to Say"

Isis is the original recycler.

She recycled her man, Osiris

And added a gold phallus

Rethink what you want to do.

ArtAmiss, "Isis"

Of my desires, whereat I weep and sing,

In joy and woe, as in a doubtful ease,

For my sweet thoughts sometime do pleasure bring:

But by and by, the cause of my disease

Gives me a pang that inwardly doth sting,

**Henry Howard, Earl of Surrey, "Alas! So All Things
Now Do Hold Their Peace"**

I touch my palm. I touch it again and again.

I leave no fingerprint. I find no white scar.

It must have been something else,

Something enormous, something too big to see.

Charles Wright, "Equation"

TRY AGAIN

Truth Lord, but I have marred them: let my shame

Go where it doth deserve.

"And know you not," says Love, "who bore the blame?"

My dear, then I will serve.

"You must sit down," says Love, "and taste my meat."

So I did sit and eat.

George Herbert, "Love"

he would rather have clean sheets,

than my poem, but as long as I don't bother her, she's glad

to know I care.

Fleda Brown, "I Write My Mother a Poem"

The rage of courts, and noise of towns;

Contented breaths his native air,

In his own grounds.

Alexander Pope, "Ode on Solitude"

I hear the bells in the sky crying, "Every being is blest."

Helen Adam, "Margaretta's Rime"

The leaves fall early this autumn, in wind.

The paired butterflies are already yellow with August

Over the grass in the West garden;

They hurt me.

Li Po, translated by Ezra Pound, "The River Merchant's Wife"

What signature shapes the vector of breath

Flowing outward?

Diane Di Prima, "The Doctor of Signatures"

And, better yet when the night is over

she can curl right up in her dress and go to sleep.

ArtAmiss, "What Does It Matter?"

For the river at Wheeling, West Virginia,

Has only two shores:

The one in hell, the other

In Bridgeport, Ohio.

**James Wright, "In Response To a Rumor That the Oldest
Whorehouse in Wheeling, West Virginia,
Has Been Condemned"**

The ceremony of innocence is drowned;

The best lack all conviction, while the worst

Are full of passionate intensity.

William Butler Yeats, "The Second Coming"

We are but farmers of ourselves, yet may,

If we can stocke ourselves, and thrive, uplay

Much, much deare treasure for the great rent day.

John Donne, "To Mr. Rowland Woodward"

Fade far away, dissolve, and quite forget

What thou among the leaves hast never known

The weariness, the fever, and the fret.

John Keats, "Ode to a Nightingale"

Twilight and evening bell,

And after that the dark!

And may there be no sadness of farewell,

When I embark.

Alfred Lord Tennyson, "Crossing the Bar"

If You wish me to leap joyfully,

Let me see You dance and sing—

Then I will leap into Love—

And from Love into Knowledge,

And from Knowledge into the Harvest,

That sweetest Fruit beyond human sense.

There I will stay with You, whirling.

Mechtild of Magdeburg, "I Cannot Dance, O Lord"

THE ANSWER IS YES

The wind goes nattering on,

Gossipy, ill at ease, in the damp room it will air.

I count off the grace and stays

My life as come to, and know I want less.

Charles Wright, "April"

What you do is how you get along

What you did is all it ever means.

Robert Creely, "Places to Be"

And on that cheek, and o'er that brow,

So soft, so calm, yet eloquent,

The smiles that win, the tints that glow,

But tell of days in goodness spent,

A mind at peace with all below,

A heart whose love is innocent!

Lord Byron, "She Walks in Beauty"

Just more waiting, with bells on,

And that Truth, is it only the FACT of WAITING,

the flash at the end.

Elise Cowen, "Did I Go Mad?"

I said to God, "I will always be unless you cease to Be,"

and my Beloved replied, "And I would cease to Be if you died."

Saint Theresa of Avila

And the more souls who resonate together,

the greater the intensity of their love,

and, mirror-like, each soul reflects the other.

Dante, "Italy"

Where God has built his blazing throne,

Nor yet alone in earth below,

With belted seas that come and go,

And endless isles of sunlit green,

Is all thy Maker's glory seen.

Oliver Wendell Holmes, "The Living Temple"

The generations labor to possess

And grave by grave we civilize the ground.

Louis Simpson, "To the Western World"

Now you feel how nothing clings to you; your vast shell
reaches into endless space, and there the rich, thick fluids
rise and flow.

Rainer Maria Rilke

Your job is to find out what the world is trying to be.

William Stafford, "Vocation"

Presently my soul grew stronger,

Hesitating then no longer.

Edgar Allan Poe, "The Raven

I encourage blossoms to flourish with ripening fruits.

Hildegard of Bingen

There, in the windless night-time,

The wanderer, marveling why,

Halts on the bridge to hearken

How soft the poplars sigh.

A.E. Housman, "A Shropshire Lad"

We play in its skeletal maze to find

A warm rabbit moving in a deep hole.

Louise Nayer, "Magic"

GET UP AND WALK OUT INTO THE FIRST LIGHT.

CHARLES SIMIC, "PARADISE"

I think I am going to climb back down
And open my eyes and shine.

James Wright, "Lightning Bugs Asleep in the Afternoon"

May wide and towering heaven collapse upon me in all its
bronze and terror, catastrophe to the peoples of the earth,
on that day when I no longer stand by my companions,
on that day when I cease to harry my enemies.

Theognis of Megara

He held radical light
as music in his skull: music.

A.R. Ammons, "He Held Radical Light"

All poets pass,
but poetry remains.

Alberto Blanco, "Poem Seen in a Motel Fan"

Love alters not with his brief hours and weeks,
But bears it out even to the edge of doom.

William Shakespeare, "Sonnet CXVI"

Love bade me welcome; yet my soul drew back,

Guilty of dust and sin.

George Herbert, "Love Bade Me Welcome"

Once

I saved my dreams

in a jar under my bed for a week.

Bucky Sinister, "The Little Children Whom God Hated"

I know what we call it

Most of the time.

But I have my own song for it,

And sometimes, even today,

I call it beauty.

James Wright, "Beautiful Ohio"

That wee-bit heap o' leaves an' stibble,

Has cost thee monie a weary nibble!

Robert Burns, "To a Mouse on Turning Her Up in Her Nest with the Plough, November, 1785"

Need,
and need not gratified
has helped me understand
why the suicide can do it
and the alcoholic can
transcend and thereby end
his limit.

Rod McKuen, "Sleep After the Brighton Lanes"

The secret
Of this journey is to let the wind
Blow its dust all over your body.

James Wright, "The Journey"

I have no heart for wars I can't fight
Or bombs that destroy.

Joanna McClure, "Dear Lover"

HURRY UP PLEASE IT'S TIME.

T.S. ELIOT, "THE WASTELAND"

The age

Requires this task:

Create

A different image:

Re-animate

The mask.

Dudley Randal, "A Different Image"

All that we see or seem

Is but a dream within a dream.

Edgar Allen Poe, "A Dream Within a Dream"

Keep walking, though there's no place to get to.

Rumi

I became You, Lord, and forgot You.

Mahadeviyakka

There's no way out.

You were born to waste your life.

You were born to this middleclass life.

Louis Simpson, "In the Suburbs"

Love me in the lightest part,

Love me in full being.

Elizabeth Barrett Browning, "A Man's Requirements"

What does not perish

Lives in thee.

Kenneth Patchen, "There Is Nothing False In Thee"

DON'T WAIT

Futile the winds

To a heart in port—

Done with the compass,

Done with chart.

Emily Dickinson, "Wild Nights—Wild Nights!"

Even in the black waters there is the luminescence

of one who has been saved.

Louise Nayer, "In the Islands"

We shall remember, when our hair is white,

These clouded days revealed in radiant light.

**George Orwell, "Our Minds are Married But We
are Too Young"**

The state of man does change and vary,

Now sound, now sick, now blyth, now sary,

William Dunbar, "Lament for the Makers"

LET THE NIGHT BEE TOO DARK FOR ME TO SEE INTO THE FUTURE. LET WHAT WILL BE, BE.

ROBERT FROST, "ACCEPTANCE"

It is not fitted with a brake,

And endless are my verses,

Nor any yarn I start to make

Appropriately terse is.

Edward Dyson, "My Typewriter"

The Strangler's ear is alert for the names of Orpheus,

Cuchulian, Gawain, and Odysseus...

Kenneth Koch, "Fresh Air"

My first love gave me singing.

My second eyes to see,

But oh, it was my third love

Who gave my soul to me.

Sara Teasdale, "Gifts"

Once my life is Your gesture,

how can I pray?

Mahadeviyakka

Don't panic

Just keep it organic.

Diamond Dave Whitaker

Wild men who caught and sang the sun in flight,

And learn, too late, they grieved it on its way,

Do not go gentle into that good night.

Dylan Thomas, "Do Not Go Gentle Into That Good Night"

Sometimes you want

A vaguer touch: I understand and won't give assertion up.

A.R. Ammons, "Working with Tools"

LOVE RULES

Nothing will be the same as once it was.

Weldon Kess, "Robinson"

A chorus of smiles, a winter morning.
Placed in a puzzling light, and moving,
Our days put on such reticence
These accents seem their own defense.

John Ashbery, "Some Trees"

The calm hand holds more than baskets of goods
from the market.

St. John of the Cross

My mother's countenance
Could not unfrown itself.

Theodore Roethke, "My Papa's Waltz"

One hour with thee! When sun is set,
Oh, what can teach me to forget
The thankless labors of the day.

Sir Walter Scott, "An Hour with Thee"

The darkness from the darkness.

Pain comes from the darkness

And we call it wisdom. It is pain.

Randall Jarrell, "90 North"

A basis rock-like of love & friendship

For all this world-wide madness seems to be needed.

John Berryman, "Of Suicide"

My roots are brandish'd in the heavens,
my fruits in earth beneath.

Surge, foam and labour into life, first born and first consum'd!

William Blake, "Europe: A Prophecy Pendulum"

Illuminated in your infinite peace, a billion stars go
spinning through the night

Rainer Maria Rilke

In a hummingbird's dance there is no bird,
only movement.

Ok-Koo Kang Grosjean, "A Hummingbird's Dance"

No love

No compassion

No intelligence

No beauty

No humility

Twenty-seven years is enough

Elise Cowen, "Unnamed"

No one worth possessing

Can be quite possessed

Sara Teasdale, "Advice to a Girl"

IT IS MADNESS

SAYS REASON

IT IS WHAT IT IS

SAYS LOVE.

ERICH FRIED, "WHAT IT IS"

Let be be final of seem.

The only emperor is the emperor of ice cream.

Wallace Stevens, "The Emperor of Ice Cream"

And the angel in the gate, the flowering plum,

Dances like Italy, imagining red.

Louis Simpson, "Walt Whitman At Bear Mountain"

We think by feeling. What is there to know?

I hear my being dance from ear to ear

I wake to sleep, and take my waking slow.

Theodore Roethke, "The Waking"

Outside the open window

The morning air is all awash with angels.

Richard Wilbur, "Love Calls Us to the Things of this World"

Where has fail'd a perfect return, indifferent of lies or
the truth?

Is it upon the ground, or in water or fire? or in the spirit of
man? or in the meat and blood?

Walt Whitman, "All Is Truth"

You have forty-nine days between death and
rebirth if you're a Buddhist.

Even the smallest soul could swim.

Maxine Kumin, "In the Park"

MAYBE

Millions of observers guess all the
time, but each person, once, can say, "Sure."

William Stafford, "My Father: October 1942"

Let it go inside of me
and touch God.
Don't be shy, dear.
Every aspect of Light we are meant
to know.

St. John of the Cross

That night of time under the Christward shelter:
I am the long world's gentleman, he said.
And share my bed with Capricorn and Cancer.

Dylan Thomas, "Altar-wise by Owl-Light

Never seek to tell thy love,
Love that never told can be.

William Blake "Never Seek to Tell Thy Love"

Love likes a gander, and adores a goose.

Theodore Roethke, "I Knew a Woman"

Don't try to see through the distances.

That's not for human beings.

Rumi

A poem spread

Across the Universe

To divine a prophecy

And affirm your dream.

Brad Olsen, "speed poem, part 2"

Let me see, then, what thereat is, and this mystery explore,

Let my heart be still a moment and this mystery explore.

Edgar Allan Poe, "The Raven"

THE ANSWER IS YES

O, may it be that far within
My inmost soul there lies
A spirit-sky, that opens with
Those voices of surprise?

William C. Gannett, "Listening for God"

If you can't be interesting at least you can be a legend

Frank O'Hara, "Yesterday Down At the Canal"

The cross is up with its crying victim, the clouds
Cover the sun, we learn a new way to lose.

Elizabeth Jennings, "Friday"

And I see you and you're divine
and I see you and you're a divine animal
and you're beautiful.

Lenore Kandel, "Hard Core Love: To Whom It Does Concern"

And the man who feels superior to others,
that man cannot dance, the real dance.

St. John of the Cross

Ah, when to the heart of man

Was it ever less than a treason

To go with the drift of things,

To yield with a grace to reason,

And bow and accept the end

Of a love or a season?

Robert Frost, "Reluctance"

the core directed to its essence.

ruth weiss, "Something Current"

Who lives in these dark houses?

I am suddenly aware

I might live here myself.

Louis Simpson, "After Midnight"

EVERYTHING CHANGES

O, unto the pine-wood At noon of day

Come with me now, Sweet love, away.

James Joyce, "Chamber Music"

I'd ne'er entangle

My heart with other fere,

Although I mangle

My joy by staying here.

Arnaut Daniel, "When Sere Leaf Falleth"

My hand knows a thing of two

(remember what turned the wheel? What melted away?)

I can ask it to pluck a rose,

I can ask it to try the doors of mystery.

John Malcolm Brinnin, "John Without Heaven"

I see, in evening air,

How slowly dark comes down on what we do.

Theodore Roethke, "In Evening Air"

A woman like that is misunderstood. I have been her kind.

Anne Sexton, "Her Kind"

Imagine it, a Sophocles complete,

The lost epic of Homer, including no doubt.

His notes, his journals, and his observations

On blindness.

Theodore Weiss, "The Fire at Alexandria"

We speak the literal to inspire

The understanding of a friend.

Robert Frost, "Revelation"

God blooms from the shoulder of the elephant

who becomes courteous to the ant.

Hafiz

How is this possible? How?

Because divine love cannot defy its very self.

Divine love will be eternally true to its own being,

and its being is giving all it can,

at the perfect moment.

Meister Eckhart, "To See As God Sees"

No one saw your ghostly

Imaginary lover

State through the window,

And tighten

The scarf at his throat.

Robert Lowell, "The Old Flame"

THE CALM SOUL KNOWS MORE THAN ANYTHING THIS WORLD CAN OFFER FROM HER BEAUTIFUL WOMB.

ST. JOHN OF THE CROSS

It is most true that the eyes are formed to serve
The inward light, and that the heavenly part.

Sir Philip Sidney, "From Astrophil and Stella"

Need is not quite belief.

Anne Sexton, "With Mercy for the Greedy"

My friend, the things that do attain
The happy life be these, I find:
The riches left, not got with pain;
The fruitful ground; the quiet mind

Henry Howard, Earl of Surrey, "My Friend, the Things That Do Attain"

If it but be a world of agony.—
"Whence camest though & whither goest thou?
How did thy course begin," I said, "and why?"

Percy Bysshe Shelley, "The Triumph of Life"

For only cool techniques
Can forge the blue-sheened steel
And train the sword-arm's skill.

Robert Conquest, "Art and Civilization"

What a gush of euphony voluminously wells!
How it swells!
How it dwells
On the Future! how it tells
Of the rapture that impels
To the swinging and the ringing
Of the bells, bells, bells...

Edgar Allan Poe, "The Bells"

If such a tincture, such a touch,
So firm a longing can impour,
Shall thy own image think it much
To watch for thy appearing hour?

Henry Vaughan, "Cock-Crowing"

Except the bee
Who in its
Gluttony drank
All the toxic
Honey

Nic Meacham, "untitled"

Thy vows are all broken,
And light is thy fame.

Lord Byron, "When We Two Parted"

Tell fortune of her blindness;
Tell nature of decay;
Tell friendship of unkindness;
Tell justice of delay.

Sir Walter Raleigh, "The Lie"

TRY AGAIN

He knew it, instantly.
He consented, himself, to
The finality of
An event.

Margaret Avison, "For Tinkers Who Travel on Foot"

In the groves of Africa from their natural wonder
The wildebeest, zebra, the okapi, the elephant,
Have entered the marvelous.
No greater marvelous
Know I than the mind's
Natural jungle.

Robert Duncan, "An African Elegy"

Make feast therefore now all this live long day,
This day for ever to me holy is,
Poure out the wine without restraint or stay,
Poure not by cups, but by the belly full.

Edmund Spenser, "Epithalamion"

If through the effect we drag the cause,
Dissect, divide, anatomize,
Results are lost in loathsome laws,
And all the ancient beauty dies.

Robert Lord Lytton, "The Artist"

Truth may seem, but cannot be,
Beauty brag, but 'tis not she,
Truth and Beauty buried be.

William Shakespeare, "The Phoenix and Turtle"

But words came halting forth wanting Invention's stay;

Invention, Nature's child, fled step-dame Study's blows,

And others' feet still seemed but strangers in my way.

Thus great with child to speak, and helpless in my throes,

"Fool," said my muse to me, "look in thy heart and write."

Sir Philip Sidney, "From Astrophil and Stella"

Some winter nights impel us to take in

Whatever lopes outside, beastly or kind.

William Meredith, "On Falling Asleep by Firelight"

Venemous thorns that are so sharp and keen

Bear flowers, we see, full fresh and

fair of hue:

Poison is also put in medicine,

And unto man his health doth oft renew.

Sir Thomas Wyatt, "Pleasure Mixed with Pain"

THE ANSWER IS NO

Think of the still and the flowing.

Edwin Honig, "November Through a Giant Copper Branch"

Sometime during eternity

Some guy shows up.

Lawrence Ferlinghetti, "Sometime During Eternity"

I tell myself.—It's dark here on the peak, and keeps on
getting darker.

It seems I am experiencing a kind of ecstasy.

Weldon Kess, "Robinson"

You could say

we live in

a life vest mentality

swim for life.

Anne Waldman, "I Am the Guard"

I am the breeze that nurtures all green.

Hildegard of Bingen

There is value

Underneath

The gold and silver

In my teeth.

W.D. Snodgrass, "April Inventory"

I planted you and I will pluck you
When it's time, said the Lord.

Mary Fabili. "From the Lord and Shingles"

If evil did not exist
She would create it.

W.D. Snodgrass

The glories of our blood and state
Are shadows, not substantial things,
There is no armour against fate,
Death lays his icy hand on Kings.

James Shirley, "Dirge"

THE TIME IS RIGHT

We breathe and
don't breathe, lie, pass in the hall, fall
into our arms, live again gone soon.

Hettie Jones, "Welcome to Our Crowd"

Please call me by true names,

So I can wake up.

And so the door of my heart can be left open.

The door of compassion.

Thich Nhat Hahn

GATHER YE ROSEBUDS WHILE YE MAY,

OLD TIME IS STILL A-FLYING

AND THIS SAME FLOWER THAT SMILES TODAY

TOMORROW WILL BE DYING.

ROBERT HERRICK, "TO THE VIRGINS, TO MAKE MUCH OF TIME"

Every morning I forget how it is.

I watch the smoke mount

In great strides above the city.

I belong to no one.

Charles Simic, "Poem"

You ask

Why I perch

On a jade green mountain?

Li Po

No virtue can be thought to have priority
Over this endeavor to preserve one's being.

W.D. Snodgrass, "After Experience Taught Me"

I saw Eternity the other night:
Like a great ring of pure and endless light,
All calm as it was bright.

Henry Vaughan, "The World"

when they scraped me clean of you
i pretended
i had done this before.

perine parker, "abortive reasoning"

I swear the earth shall surely be complete to him
or her who shall be complete.

Walt Whitman, "A Song of the Rolling Earth"

THE ANSWER IS MOST DEFINITELY

Come live with me and be my love,
And we will come new pleasures prove,
Of golden sands and crystal brooks,
With silken lines and silver hooks.

John Donne, "The Bait"

Once drinking deep of the divinest anguish,

How could I seek the empty world again?

Emily Bronte, "Remembrance"

I would I could adopt your will,

See with your eyes, and set my heart

Beating by yours.

Robert Browning, "Two in the Campagna"

O hell! what do mine eyes with grief behold?

Gary Snyder, "Milton by Firelight"

Ask me no more where those starres light,

That downwards fall in the dead of night;

For in your eyes they sit, and there,

Fix'ed become as in their sphere.

Thomas Carew, "Song"

I would rather thou shouldst painfully repent,

Than by my threatenings rest still innocent.

John Donne, "The Apparition"

Pure of heart! thou needest not ask of me

What this strong music in the soul may be!

Samuel Taylor Coleridge, "Dejections: An Ode"

The day we die

The wind comes down

To take away

Our footprints.

Southern Bushmen, "The Way We Die"

Wet your whistle with wine now, for the dog star, wheeling up the sky,

brings back the summer, the time all things are parched under the searing heat.

Alcaeus of Mytilene, "Winter Scene"

Of the wide world I stand alone, and think

Till love and fame to nothingness do sink.

John Keats, "When I Have Fears That I May Cease to Be"

Music, when soft voices die,

Vibrates in the memory.

Percy Bysshe Shelley, "Music, When Soft Voices Die"

OUTCOME LIKELY

Wait upon it for
The edge only it gives.

Joanna McClure, "Hard Edge"

Beautiful and wild, the hawks, and men
that are dying, remember him.

Robinson Jeffers, "Hurt Hawks"

Even such is time, which takes in trust

Our youth, our joys, and all we have,

And pays us but with age and dust,

Who in the dark and silent grave

When we have wandered all our ways

Shuts up the story of our days,

And from which earth, and grave, and dust

The lord shall raise me up, I trust.

Sir Walter Raleigh, "The Author's Epitaph, Made by Himself"

Nothing is free and in this truth lies the reality
that freedom is nothingness.

Nic Meacham, "Free"

These two were rapid falcons in a snare,

Condemned to do the flitting of the bat.

George Meredith, "Thus Piteously Love Close What He Begat"

I grow old... I grow old...

I shall wear the bottoms of my trousers rolled.

Thomas Stearns Eliot," The Love Song of J. Alfred Prufrock"

When we would go moving

as people do with purpose

would take apart this room stone by stone

and set ourselves outdoors

to mate with the sun.

Mary Norbert Korte, "The Room Within"

WHAT IS THIS LIFE IF, FULL OF CARE,

WE HAVE NO TIME TO STAND AND STARE.

WILLIAM HENRY DAVIES, "LEISURE"

Twelve nations

Bleed. Because I love, because

I need cherries, I cannot help them.

My happiness, bought cheap, must last forever.

Lucien Stryk, "Cherries"

I am the rain coming from the dew that causes the
grasses to laugh with joy of life.

Hildegard of Bingen

There, like the wind through woods in riot,

Through him the gale of life blew high.

Alfred Edward Housman, "On Wenlock Edge"

With bars they blur the gracious moon,

And blind the goodly sun:

And they do well to hide their Hell,

For in it things are done.

Oscar Wilde, "The Ballad of Reading Gaol"

CONFIDENTLY PROCEED

Out of me unworthy and unknown
The vibrations of deathless music.

Edgar Lee Masters, "Anne Rutledge"

When the mind becomes
Your mind, what is left to remember?

Mahadeviyakka
Better by far you should forget and smile
Than that you should remember and be sad.

Christina Georgina Rossetti, "Remember"

But like everyone else I learned
each time nothing new, only that
as it were, a music, however harsh, that held us
however loosely, had stopped, and left
a heavy thick silence in its place.

Denise Levertov, "The Dead"

what well have you crawled out of
what wall have you recalled

perine parker, "backsliding daughters"

From perfect grief there need not be
Wisdom or even memory.

Dante Gabriel Rossetti, "The Woodspurge"

But fly our paths, our feverish contact fly!
For strong the infection of our mental strife.

Matthew Arnold, "The Scholar-Gipsy"

After hours of giddy drinking and wild abandon
she found herself under the table
in only her shoes!

ArtAmiss, "The Gift Bag"

And the ground spoke when she was born.

**Joy Harjo, "For Alva Benson, and for Those Who Have
Learned to Speak"**

Who hath not learned, in hours of faith,
The truth to flesh and sense unknown,
That life is ever lord of Death,
And Love can never lose its own!

John Greenleaf Whittier, "Snow Bound; A Winter Idyl"

There she weaves by night and day
A magic web with colours gay.

Alfred Lord Tennyson, "The Lady of Shallot"

It isn't true about the lambs. They are not meek.

Alice B. Fogel, "The Necessity"

They danced by the light of the moon,
The moon,
The moon,
They danced by the light of the moon.

Edward Lear, "The Owl and the Pussycat"

FORGIVE

Shape nothing, lips; be lovely-dumb.

Gerard Manley Hopkins, "The Habit of Perfection"

Every day I wake far away
from my life, in a foreign country.

Louis Simpson, "American Dreams"

Powered by words,

a company of voices.

In a fury he spins himself

turning upon the spit of his own burning rays,

and in a passion sings the room ablaze.

Madeline Gleason, "The Interior Castle"

When the bonny blade carouses,

Pockets are full, and spirits high,

What are acres? What are houses?

Only dirt, or wet or dry.

Samuel Johnson, "A Short Song of Congratulation"

LITTLE THINK'ST THOU

THAT THOU TO-MORROW,

ERE THAT SUN DOTH WAKE,

MUST WITH THIS SUN,

AND ME A JOURNEY TAKE.

JOHN DONNE, "THE BLOSSOME"

The living record of your memory.

'Gainst death and all-obvious enmity

Shall you pace forth; your praise shall still find room

Even in the eyes of all prosperity

That wear this world out to the ending doom.

So, till the judgment that yourself arise,

You live in this, and dwell in lovers' eyes.

William Shakespeare, "Sonnet 55"

Knowledge always deceives.

It always limits the Truth, every concept and image does.

Meister Eckhart

The sun may set and rise:

But we contrarywise

Sleep after our short light

One everlasting night.

Sir Walter Raleigh, "From the History of the World"

All extremes must meet;

As some old poet has said:

Out of a little earth

And heaven, was Adam made.

Madeline Gleason, "Lyrics"

BE TRUE

This morning I learned

There are no birds in Guam.

How come?

Mary Fabili, "From Second Monday in May 1988"

Men at forty

Learn to close softly

The doors to rooms they will not be

Coming back to.

Donald Justice, "Men At Forty"

SUTTER MARIN swam in PLAYA ANGEL

made a pact with the angels all mad to be reborn.

ruth weiss, "Post-card 1995"

Fearing making guilt making shame

Making fantasy and logic and game and

Elegance of covering splendour

Emptying memory of the event.

Elise Cowen, "Teacher—Your Body My Kabbalah"

All you need to do is
Look good, and show a little skin.

Jessyka Stinston, "Vine Goddess"

Ill fares the land, to hastening ills a prey,
Where wealth accumulates and men decay.

Oliver Goldsmith, "The Deserted Village"

Man is all symmetrie
Full of proportions, one limbe to another,
And all to all the world besides:
Each part may call the farthes, brother.

George Herbert, "Man"

DON'T WAIT

Perhaps that's how
It's supposed to be?

Charles Simic, "Toy Factory"

A rain of tears, a cloud of dark disdain,
Hath done the wearied cords great hinderance.

Sir Thomas Wyatt the Elder, "My Galley"

Who on Love's seas more glorious wouldst appear?

Like untuned golden strings all women are,

Which long time lie untouched, will harshly jar.

Vessels of brass, oft handled, brightly shine.

Christopher Marlowe, "Hero and Leander"

Only that Illumined One

Who keeps

Seducing the formless into form

Had the charm to win my heart.

Hafiz

She ran away in everybody's dreams calling out like a booming
flame running running into the lines

of bards and lions lovers and birds running with her arms out
wide into the bright flapping dark.

**Norbert Korte, "Eddie Mae the Cook Dreamed Sister Mary Ran
Off with Allen Ginsberg"**

He loves to sit and hear me sing,

Then, laughing, sports and plays with me;

Then stretches out my golden wing,

And mocks my loss of liberty.

William Blake, "How Sweet I Roam'd from Field to Field"

"In my youth," father William replied to his son,

"I feared it might injure the brain;

But, now that I'm perfectly sure I have none,

Why, I do it again and again."

Lewis Carroll, "You Are Old, Father William"

Be still, I am content,

Take back your poor compassion

Joy was a flame in me

Too steady to destroy.

Sara Teasdale, "The Answer"

To your eyes, ears, and tongue, and every part.

If then your body go, what need you a heart?

John Donne, "The Blossom"

> # IN THE END THE DEVIL
> # HE ALWAYS WINS
> # YOU THINK YOU CAN OUT RUN HIM
> # BUT LORD HOW HE CAN SWIM.
>
> ## A. RAE, "HEED"

True love in every moment praises God.

Longing love brings a sorrow sweet to the pure.

Seeking love belongs to itself alone.

Understanding love gives itself equally to all.

Enlightened love is mingled with the sadness of the world.

Mechtild of Magdeburg

Sad true lover never find my grave
To weep there.

William Shakespeare, "Twelfth Night"

I laugh

But say

Nothing

My heart

Free

Like a peach blossom

Li Po

Live television of what—is a lie.

Charles Olson, "A Later Note On Letter #15"

Exterminator does his job, takes his money, leaves.
In the long run of things, he knows who will survive.

Lucien Stryk, "Exterminator"

But don't worry!
What must come, comes.
Face everything with love,
as your mind dissolves in God.

Lal Ded, translated by Coleman Barks

One word is too often profaned For me to profane it,
One feeling too falsely disdained For thee to disdain it.

Percy Bysshe Shelley, "One Word Is Too Often Profaned"

The night knows nothing of the chants of night
It is what it is as
I am what I am.

Wallace Stevens

And lives go on.
And lives go on.
Like sudden lights
At street corners.

Donald Justice, "Bus Stop"

I love the dark race of poets,
And yet there is also happiness. Happiness,
If I can stand it, I can stand anything.

Louis Simpson, "Luminous Night"

If all the world and love were young,
And truth in every shepherd's tongue,
These pretty pleasure might me move
To live with thee, and be thy love.

Sir Walter Raleigh, "The Nymph's Reply"

DON'T DOUBT YOURSELF

I am led by the spirit to feed the purest streams.

Hildegard of Bingen

And that each thing exactly represents itself,
and what has preceded it.

Walt Whitman, "All Is Truth"

And now we talk of the "inner life,"
And I ask myself, where is it?

Louis Simpson, "The Silent Piano"

If you have a spirit, lose it.
Lose it to return where with one word,
we came from.
Now, thousands of words, and we refuse to leave.

Rumi

Not marble, nor the gilded monuments
Of princes shall outlive this powerful rhyme;
But you shall shine more bright in these contents
Than unswept stone besmeared with sluttish time.

William Shakespeare, "Sonnet LV"

That I, above all, am chosen—even I
Must find that strange. I who was always
Disobedient, rebellious—smoked in the dining car.

W.D. Snodgrass, "The Fuhrer Bunker"

The whimpering airs that cry by night and never
find their rest
Are sobbing to be taken in and soothed upon my breast.

Enid Derham, "The Wind-Child"

THE HEAVENS SAY YES

How did the rose ever open its heart
and give to this world all of its beauty?

It felt the encouragement of light against its being,
otherwise we all remain too frightened.

Hafiz

But where is he, the Pilgrim of my song,

The being who upheld it through the past?

**Lord Byron, CLXIV, from "Canto the Fourth, Childe
Harold's Pilgrimage"**

I admit to being, at times,

Suddenly, and without the slightest warning,

Exceedingly happy.

Charles Simic, "Heights of Folly"

I have always been at the same time

woman enough to be moved to tears

and man enough

to drive my car in any direction.

Hettie Jones, "Teddy Bears on the Highway"

When the mind is consumed with remembrance of Him
something divine happens to the heart that shapes
the hand and tongue

and eye into the word Love.

Hafiz

From cage to cage the caravan moves, but I give thanks,
for at each divine juncture my wings expand and I touch
Him more intimately.

Meister Eckhart

Love touches love

the temple and the god are one.

Lenore Kandel, "God/Love Poem"

Best of all is to be idle,

And especially on a Thursday,

And to sip wine while studying the light.

Charles Simic, "Against Whatever It Is That's Encroaching"

IT'S YOUR LAST CHANCE

Each creature God made must live in its own true nature;

How could I resist my nature, that lives for oneness with God?

Mechtild of Magdeburg

Love alters not with his brief hour and weeks,

But bears it out even to the edge of doom.

William Shakespeare, "Sonnets CXVI"

And an old woman with a witch's stare

Cried "Praise the Lord!"

She vanishes on a bus

With hissing air brakes, like an incubus.

Louis Simpson, "Hot Night on Water Street"

But selfless love bears an effortless fruit, working so quietly
even the body cannot say how it comes and goes.

Mechtild of Magdeburg

The miracles that magic will perform

Will make thee vow to study nothing else.

Christopher Marlowe, "Dr Faustus. Act 1"

THE ANSWER IS YES

For we support all, fuse all,

After the rest is done and gone, we remain.

Walt Whitman, "As I Walk These Broad, Majestic Days"

Shall I compare thee to a summer's day?

Thou art more lovely and more temperate.

William Shakespeare, "Sonnet 18"

But by and by the cause of my disease

Gives me a pang that inwardly doth sting,

When that I think what grief it is again

To live and lack the thing should rid my pain.

**Henry Howard, Earl of Surrey, "Alas! So All Things
Now Do Hold Their Peace"**

Bills, bills, bills

Thrills, thrills, thrills

Skills, skills, skills

Joanna McClure, "June 18, 1984"

Sometimes afraid of reunion,

Sometimes of separation:

You and I,

So fond of the notion of a you and an I,

Should live as though

we'd never heard those pronouns.

Rumi

Peace is always beautiful,

The myth of heaven indicates peace and night.

Walt Whitman, "The Sleepers"

BELIEVE

God, whose love and joy are present everywhere, can't come
to visit you unless you aren't there.

Angelus Silesius

For most men in a brazen prison live,

Where, in the sun's hot eye,

With heads bent o'er their toil, they languidly

Their lives to some unmeaning taskwork give

Matthew Arnold, "A Summer Night"

In the fire of its making,

Gold doesn't vanish:

The fire brightens.

Mechtild of Magdeburg

Thy liberality, exceeds my power,

Suffice it, that I thus record thy gifts,

And bear them treasur'd in a grateful mind!

John Milton, "To My Father"

HOPE SMILED WHEN YOUR NATIVITY WAS CAST.

WILLIAM WORDSWORTH, "FLOWERS ON THE TOP OF THE PILLARS AT THE ENTRANCE OF THE CAVE"

Be well assured that on our side

The abiding oceans fight.

Rudyard Kipling, "A Song in Storm"

As for the people—see how they neglect you!

Only a poet pauses to read the inscription.

Louis Simpson, "Walt Whitman At Bear Mountain"

Quoth the raven, "Nevermore"

Edgar Allan Poe, "The Raven"

How do I listen to others?
As if everyone were my Master
Speaking to me
His cherished last words.

Hafiz

MAYBE

Wisdom is sweeter than honey, brings
more joy than wine, illumines more
than the sun, is more precious
than jewels.

Makeda, Queen of Sheba

A flower unplucked is but left to the falling,
And nothing is gained by not gathering roses.

Robert Lee Frost, "Asking for Roses"

I knuckled under, no regrets
but I've always wondered.

Hettie Jones, "Sonnet"

Take of English earth as much
As either hand may rightly clutch.
In the taking of it breathe
Prayer for all who lie beneath.

Rudyard Kipling, "A Charm"

LOOK WITHIN

Birds make great sky-circles of their freedom.
How do they learn it?
They fall, and falling,
they're given wings.

Rumi

Love is the funeral pyre where I have laid my living body.

Hafiz

No more be grieved at that which thou hast done:
Roses have thorns, and silver fountains mud.
Clouds and eclipses stain both moon and sun,
And loathsome canker lives in sweetest bud.

William Shakespeare, "Sonnet 35"

I say them, woman-who-signifies

I light the fire

I sit like a Buddha

I feed the animals outside the door

I blow out the lamp.

Anne Waldman, "Fast Speaking Woman"

By the high verandah pillars, by the rotting bloodwood gates.

Crowded town or dreary seaboard, everywhere some
woman waits!

M. Forrest, "The Lonely Woman"

Through love, through hope, and faith's transcendent dower,

We feel that we are greater than we know.

Alfred Lord Tennyson, "After-Thought"

By the high verandah pillars, by the rotting bloodwood gates.

Crowded town or dreary seaboard, everywhere some
woman waits!

M. Forrest, "The Lonely Woman"

The Difference Between a good artist

And a great one Is:

The novice

Will often lay down his tool

Or brush

Then pick up an invisible club

On the mind's table

And helplessly smash the easels and

Jade.

Whereas the vintage man

No longer hurts himself or

Anyone and keeps on

Sculpting

Light.

Hafiz

The roses in the gypsy's window in a blue vase,
look real, as unreal.

Denise Levertov, "The Gypsy's Window"

But O! the heavy change, now thou art gone,

Now thou art gone, and never must return!

John Milton, "Lycidas"

Ironic, but one of the most intimate

acts of our body is death.

So beautiful appeared my death—knowing who
then I would kiss,

I died a thousand times before I died.

Rabia

A FISH CANNOT DROWN IN WATER, A BIRD DOES NOT FALL IN AIR.

MECHTILD OF MAGDEBURG

'Is thine own heart to thine own face affected?

Can thy right hand seize love upon thy left?

William Shakespeare, "Venus and Adonis"

And olden memories
Are startled from their long repose
Like shadows on the silent snows.

Abijah M. Ide, "To Isadore"

While the milder fates consent,
Let's enjoy our merriment.

Robert Herrick, "A Lyric to Mirth"

I bring you with reverent hands
The books of my numberless dreams

William Butler Yeats, "A Poet to His Beloved"

in egypt
they tell the days
by the strings in their beads.

ruth weiss, "The Brink"

This poem is not addressed to you.
You may come into it briefly,
But no one will find you here, no one.
You will have changed before the poem will.

Donald Justice, "Poem"

The sky is always ours,
even though we are crowded together.

Louise Nayer, "Dream of the Uninterrupted Moss"

And out-lived illusions rise,
And the soft leaves of the landscape
Open on my thoughtful eyes.

Jennings Carmichael, "An Old Bush Road"

YEARN FOR THE GOOD

Only a moment, as clocks can reckon,

Dwells the soul at that height of heights.

John Le Gay Brereton, "Middle Harbour"

And grateful, that by nature's quietness

And solitary musings, all my heart

Is softened, and made worthy to indulge

Love, and the thoughts that yearn for human kind.

Samuel Taylor Coleridge, "Fears in Solitude"

Love is that that never sleeps,

nor even rests, nor stays

for long with those that do.

Love is language

that cannot be said,

or heard.

Rumi

Only a Perfect One
Who is always laughing at the word
Two
Can make you know
Of
Love.

Hafiz, "Laughing at the Word Two"

I was delighted with myself,
having offered everything I had;
my heart my faith, my work.
"And who are you," you said,
"to think you have so much to offer?
It seems you have forgotten
where you've come from."

Rumi

You in whose ultimate madness we live,
You flinging yourself out into the emptiness,
You—like us—great an instant,
O only universe we know, forgive us.

Galway Kinnell, "On Frozen Fields"

Look to the weather bow,

Breakers are round thee;

Let fall the plummet now,

Shallows may ground thee.

Caroline Bowles Southey, "Mariner's Hymn"

The woods are lovely, dark and deep.

But I have promises to keep,

And miles to go before I sleep,

And miles to go before I sleep.

Robert Frost, "Stopping by Woods on a Snowy Evening"

All speaks of change: the renovated forms

Of long-forgotten thins arise again.

**Sir Humphry Davy, "Written After Recovery from a
Dangerous Illness"**

Such sailing and gilding,

Such sinking and sliding,

Such lofty curvetting,

And grand pirouetting

Richard Harris Barham, "The Witches' Frolic"

So for this night I linger here,

And full tossings to and fro,

Expect still when thou wilt appear

That I may get me up, and go.

Henry Vaughn, "The Pilgrimage"

PERHAPS

I shall prosper,

I shall yet remain alive.

Takelma (Oregon) "Medicine Formula"

I watched you lay your athletes body down

Across the railroad earth

To make a bridge for souls

Helen Weaver, "For Jack"

The rest of my days I spend

wandering: wondering

what, anyway,

was that sticky infusion, that rank flavor of blood,

that poetry, by which I lived?

Galway Kinnell, "The Bear"

> # DRUMSOUND RISES ON THE AIR,
> # ITS THROB, MY HEART.
> # A VOICE INSIDE THE BEAT SAYS,
> # "I KNOW YOU'RE TIRED, BUT COME.
> # THIS IS THE WAY."
> ## RUMI

There is a Power whose care
Teaches thy way along that pathless coast.

William Cullen Bryant, "To a Waterfowl"

Found a family, build a state,
The pledged event is still the same.

**Herman Melville, "Fragments of a Lost Gnostic
Poem of the 12th Century"**

Some for the Glories of This World; and some
Sigh for the Prophet's Paradise to come;
Ah, take the Cash, and let the Credit go,
Nor heed the rumble of a distant Drum!

Edward Fitzgerald, "The Rubaiyat of Omar Khayyam"

The way of love is not a subtle argument.

The door there is devastation.

Rumi

I am the self-consumer of my woes—

They rise and vanish in oblivion's host.

John Clare, "I Am"

Poetry, he don't work for the city.

He dumps your garbage onto a blank page.

You don't recognize it.

You call it beautiful.

Julia Vinograd, "From Poetry"

O, or that full bliss of though allied,

Never to mortals given,

O, la thye lovely dreams aside,

Or lift them unto heaven!

Felicia Hemans, "The Childe's Destiny"

TRY AGAIN

Again!

Come, give, yield all your strength to me!

James Joyce, "A Prayer"

For we are the same things our fathers have been;

We see the same sights that our fathers have seen.

William Knox, "Why Should the Spirit of Mortal Be Proud?"

Children can easily open the drawer that lets

the spirit rise up and wear

Its favorite

costume of mirth and laughter.

Hafiz

We know nothing until we know everything.

St. Catherine of Siena

Insects on a bough floating downriver, still singing.

Issa, "In This World"

There is a garden in her face,

Where roses and white lilies grow;

A heavenly paradise is that place,

Wherein all pleasant fruits do flow.

Thomas Campian

Hail divinest Melancholy,

Whose saintly visage is too bright

To hit the sense of human sight.

John Milton, "Il Penseroso"

Now let us sport us while we may,

And now, like amorous birds of prey,

Rather at once our time devour

Than languish in his slow-chapped power.

Andrew Marvell, "To His Coy Mistress"

The lunatic, the lover, and the poet

Are of imagination all compact.

William Shakespeare, "A Midsummer Night's Dream"

It is the rain

And all the sadness in the world

Won't make it stop.

Mary Fabili, "From the Priest"

I strive to mix some gladness with my strain,

But the sad strings complain,

And will not please the ear.

James Russell Lowell, "Commemoration Ode"

ALL SIGNS POINT TO YES

Loosened from the minor's tether;

Free to mortgage or to sell.

Samuel Johnson, "A Short Song of Congratulations"

In moons and tides and weather wise,

He reads the clouds as prophecies.

John Greenleaf Whittier, "Snow-Bound; A Winter Idyl"

The still air moves, the wide room is less dim

Richard W. Gilder, "Dawn"

Cannibals love their food and don't hate anyone

Cannibals sing at the smell of dinner cooking

Listen to their happy music.

Julia Vinograd, "Cannibal Music"

I do not own an inch of land,

But all I see is mine.

Lucy Larcom, "A Strip of Blue"

Slow, slow, fresh fount, keepe time with my salt teares.

Benjamin Jonson, "Song"

What now?

any moment the question—the only answer!

ruth weiss, "Single Out"

He thought as a sage, though he felt as a man

James Beattie, "The Hermit"

My mind was once the true survey

Of all these meadows fresh and gay.

Andrew Marvell, "The Mower's Song"

I bought a rose, a red, red rose.

Put it in a bottle and threw it out to sea.

Whoever finds it, there is no map.

Julia Vinograd, "Valentine"

Silence. Ashes

in the grate. Whatever it is

that keeps us from heaven,

sloth, wrath, greed, fear,

could we only reinvent it on earth

as song.

Galway Kinnell, "Last Song"

Those mortals with whom we couple or have coupled,

Clinging to our swan-suits, our bull-skins,

Our masquerades in coin and shrubbery.

Carolyn Kizer, "The Copulating Gods"

But, present still, though now unseen,

When brightly shines the prosperous day,

Be thoughts of thee a cloudy screen,

To temper the deceitful ray.

Sir Walter Scott, "Hymn of the Hebrew Maid"

You're in my eyes.

How else could I see light?

You're in my brain.

This wild joy.

If love did not live in matter,

how would any place have any hold on anyone?

Rumi

ASK AGAIN LATER

Lord, you are my lover, my longing,

my flowing stream, my sun, and I am your reflection.

Mechthild of Magdeburg

Oh my Lord, the stars glitter and the

eyes of men are closed.

Rabi'a

He that is grounded in astrology,

Enriched with tongues, well seen in minerals,

Hath all the principles magic doth require.

Christopher Marlowe, "Dr. Faustus. Act 1"

The sea is calling, calling,

Along the hollow shore.

I know each nook in the rocky strand,

And the crimson weeds on the golden sand,

And the worn old cliff where sea-pinks cling,

And the winding caves where the echoes ring.

Unknown, "The Fisherman's Summons"

Content I live; this is my stay,—

I seek no more than my suffice.

I press to bear no haughty sway;

Look, what I lack my mind supplies.

William Byrd, "My Mind to Me a Kingdom Is"

By the distant rill the maple grove looks scattered;

By the deep mountain the lane of bamboos looks peaceful;

The thin mist swallows up the departing birds;

The thin mist of the sinking sun companions the homing cattle.

Yuan Hao-wen, "The Maple Grove"

But flattery never seems absurd;

The flattered always takes your word.

John Gay, "The Painter Who Pleased Nobody and Everybody"

Even after all this time
the sun never says to the earth,
"You owe me."
Look what happens
with a love like that—it lights the whole world.

Hafiz

Ask the animals, and they will teach you.
Ask the birds of air, and they will tell you.

Job 12:7-10, "Ask the Animals"

Ever let the fancy roam,
Pleasure never is at home.

John Keats, "Fancy"

In the summer rain,
the path has disappeared

Buson, "Green Leaves, White Water"

No one yet had invented ownership
Nor guilt nor time.

Lenore Kandel, "Enlightenment Poem"

Her lips began to scorch,

That juice was wormwood to her tongue,

She loathed the feast

Christina Rossetti, "Goblin Market"

You can never bring in a wall.

William Shakespeare, "A Midsummer Night's Dream"

Listen my children and you shall hear

The sound of your own steps

The sound of your hereafter

Patti Smith, "Notes for the Future"

Ah, not to be cut off,

not through the slightest partition

shut out from the law of the stars.

Rainer Maria Rilke

WHAT YOU DESIRE WILL BE YOURS

down the open hatch again you silly liquid sap

perine parker, "with daddy"

I plucked pink blossoms from mine apple-tree
And wore them all that evening in my hair:
Then in due season when I went to see I found no
apples there.

Christina Rossetti, "An Apple Gathering"

One need not be a chamber to be haunted.

Emily Dickinson, "Ghosts"

Goddess's of Air, Isis, and Athena
They will help you know that you are.

ArtAmiss, "fortune"

As though at hide-and-seek with Spring.
My inmost thoughts, who can know them?
Ties of friendship are hard to make.
Alone in my romance, alone in my fragrance,
The moon comes to look for me.

Chu Tun-ju, "A Single Plum Tree"

Each new discovery as
Slow and quiet as a
Possum's front feet.

Joanna McClure, "Collage"

From a world composed, closed to us,

back to nowhere, the north.

Denise Levertov, "Another Journey"

My Beloved is a steeped herb, he has cured me of life.

Mira belongs to Giridhara, the One who lifts all,

and everyone says she is mad.

Mira

Observe your life, between two breaths.

Breath is a wind, both coming and going.

On this wind you have built your life—

but how will a castle rest on a cloud?

Avicenna (Ibn Sina)

Dwell thou in endless

Light, discharged soul.

Sir Henry Wotton, "Tears at the Grave of Sr. Albertus Morton"

Now, when he and I meet, after all these years,

I say to the bitch inside me, don't start growling.

Carolyn Kizer, "Bitch"

Love is the funeral pyre
where the heart
must lay its body.

Hafiz, "Persia"

He who the sword of heaven will bear
Should be as holy as severe

William Shakespeare, "Measure for Measure"

I want to burn here, in the heart of the flame,
in the middle of your arms, under the sun.

Katherine O'Brien, "untitled"

When the soul lies down in that grass, the world is
too full to talk about.

Rumi, translated by John Moyne and Coleman Barks

Now this day you have ceased to see daylight.
Think only of what is good.
Do not think of anything uselessly.

Fox, "A Speech to the Dead"

What has risen

From the tangled web of thought and sinew

now shines with jubilation

through the eyes of angels

and screams from the guts of Infinite existence

Itself.

Hafiz

The little tress, ownerless, blossom untended;

Above the waste of misty grass the ravens home for the night.

Here and there broken walls encircle ancient wells;

Erstwhile, each of these was someone's habitation.

Tai Fu-Ku, "The Little Peach Trees"

Should we our Sorrows in this Method range,

Oft as Misfortune doth their Subjects change.

Henry King, "An Elegy Upon My Best Friend"

Time shall moult away his wings

Ere he shall discover

In the whole wide world again

Such a constant Lover.

Sir John Suckling

If you live on the breath,

you won't be tortured
by hunger and thirst,
or the longing to touch.
The purpose of being born is fulfilled
in the state between "I am"
and "That."

Lalla

The nice rain knows its season,
It is born of Spring.
It follows the wind secretly into the night.
And showers its blessings, silently, softly, upon everything.

Li Po, "A Quiet Temple Thick Set With Flowers"

In this world
we walk on the roof of hell,
gazing at flowers.

Issa, "In This World"

REPLY HAZY

In the midst of plenty you have started out.

Chiricahua, "Song of Maturation"

If this belief from heaven be sent
If such be Nature's holy plan,
Have I not reason to lament
What man has made of man?

William Wordsworth, "Lines Written in Early Spring"

Oh turn away those cruel Eyes,
The stars of my undoing.

Thomas Stanley, "The Relapse"

I have lived on the lip of insanity, wanting to
know reasons, knocking on a door. It opens.
I've been knocking from the inside!

Rumi, translated by John Moyne and Coleman Barks

Palate, the hutch of tasty lust,
Desire not to be rinsed with wine.

Gerard Manley Hopkins, "The Habit of Perfection"

Their father the Sun
who brought them to life
spoke the word of taking us out

Zuni, "The Beginning, Part 1" translated by Dennis Tedlock

To place You in my heart may turn You into thought.

I will not do that!

To hold You with my eyes may turn You into thorn.

I will not do that!

I will set You on my breath

So You will become my life.

Rumi, translated by Maryam Mafi & Azima Melita Kolin

Kings have locked their doors and

each lover is alone with his love.

Here, I am alone with You.

Rabi'a

But do not touch my heart, and so be gone;

Strike deep thy burning arrow in.

Abraham Cowley, "The Request"

Every man to the devil his own way

Every man to the devil he must go.

Lizzy Lee Savage, "Every Man to the Devil His Own Way"

He fumbles at your spirit

As players at the keys.

Emily Dickinson, "The Master"

Here is my aphorism of the day:
Happy people are monogamous,
Even in California.
So how does the poem play.

Carolyn Kizer, "Afternoon Happiness"

Listen, if you can stand to.
Union with the Friend means not being who you've been,
being instead silence: A place: A view
where language is inside seeing.

Rumi

Any thought of release from this life
will wrap you only more tightly in its snares.

Ly Ngoc Kiev

Is it for me to drink the sweet water poured out
And all day sit idle?

Papago, "War Song"

You look but cannot reach,
You walk, the road twisting.

Sung Dynasty, "Moments of Riding Mist"

Know the true nature of your Beloved.

In His loving eyes your every thought,

word, and movement is always,

always beautiful.

Hafiz

Cut brambles long enough, sprout after sprout,

and the lotus will bloom of

its own accord:

Already waiting in the clearing, the single image of light.

The day you see this, that day you will become it.

Sun Bu-er

Know that love is a careless child

And forgets promise past.

**Anonymous, "As You Came from the Holy Land
of Walsingham"**

Wearing our gestures, how wise you grow,

ballooning to overfill our space,

the almost-parents of your parents now.

So briefly having you back to measure us

is harder than having let you go.

Maxine Kumin, "Family Reunion"

Not one is dissatisfied—not one is demented
with the mania of owning things.

Walt Whitman, "The Beasts"

YOU MAY RELY ON IT

You are sufficient.
You are perfect wherever you are.
When powerful your splendor overflows
My eyes you little heaven.

Hyonsung Kim, "Light"

May it be beautiful before me.
May it be beautiful behind me.
May it be beautiful below me.
May it be beautiful above me.
May it be beautiful all around me.
In beauty it is finished.

Navajo, "A Prayer of the Night Chant"

One hundred and sixty-five recycled coffee filters.
A lot of time And a lot of glue.

Debbie Dean, "Sex Spresso"

My Love to Saints and Angels, things divine,

But in thy tender jealousy dost doubt

Least the World, Fleshe, yea Devill putt thee out.

John Donne, "Holy Sonnets, 17"

Joy may you have, and gentle heart's content.

Edmund Spenser, Prothalamion

There is danger where I move my feet. I am whirlwind.

Navajo, "Song of the Black Bear"

The sleeping person looks for a Buddha, the troubled person
turns toward meditation.

Ly Ngoc Kiev

Find also in this sound a thought,

Hearing it by this distant northern sea.

Matthew Arnold, "Dover Beach"

You speak to me of dangers that I may fear,

But I have willed to go, my friends.

Osage, "A Warrior's Song of Defiance"

May your road be fulfilled.

Reaching to the road of your sun father,

When your road is fulfilled,

In your thoughts may we live.

Zuni, "Prayer Spoken While Presenting An Infant to the Sun"

The inner-what is it?

if not intensified sky,

hurled through with birds and deep

with the wind of homecoming.

Rainer Maria Rilke

I love her

like a mother,

and she embraces me

as her own child.

I will follow

her footprints

and she will not cast me away.

Makeda, Queen of Sheba

ALL SIGNS POINT TO NO

Mountains are steadfast but the mountain streams go by, go by, and yesterdays are like the rushing streams, they fly, they fly, and the great heroes,

famous for a day, they die, they die.

Hwang Chin

Love bade me welcome: yet my soul drew back,

Guiltie of dust and sinne.

George Herbert, "Love (III)"

Crescent moon—bent to the shape of the cold.

Issa, "In This World"

Spirits intoxicate

The drinker, not the glass.

James Merrill, "Waterspout"

This mountain of release is such that the

ascent's most painful at the start, below;

the more you rise, the milder it will be.

Dante

When shall the traveller come home,

That will not move?

Henry Vaughan, "The Resolve"

ASK AGAIN

Not one kneels to one another, nor to this kind that lived
thousands of years ago,

Not one is respectable or unhappy over the whole earth.

Walt Whitman, "I Believe a Leaf of Grass"

But the one who knows

That there's nothing to seek

Knows too that there's nothing to say.

She keeps her mouth closed.

Ly Ngoc Kiev

When the words stop and you can endure the silence that
reveals your heart's pain of emptiness or that great wrenching-
sweet longing, that is the time to

try and listen to what the Beloved's eyes most want to say.

Hafiz

THE SINGLE IMAGE OF LIGHT
THE DAY YOU SEE THIS,
THAT DAY YOU WILL BECOME IT.

SUN 'BU-ER

Out of me unworthy and unknown
The vibrations of a deathless music.

Edgar Lee Masters, "Anne Rutledge"

Wandering from room to room.
Smiling.

Joanna McClure, "Night"

No. I yearn upward, touch you close,
Then stand away. I kiss your cheek,
Catch your soul's warmth,—I pluck the rose
And love it more than tongue can speak.

Robert Browning, "Two in the Campagna"

Amid all forms visible, the spreading blades
I see as I move from place to place.

Osage, "The Song of the Maize"

And when the slope feels gentle to the point that
climbing up sheer rock is effortless
as though you were gliding downstream in a boat,
then you will have arrived where this path ends.

Dante

IT IS CERTAIN

The height of the adventure is the height
Of country where two village cultures faded
Into each other. Both of them are lost.

Robert Frost, "Directive"

And so time passes, passes by, passes over, passes away and
through and pass the butter, please. Sometimes time passes
by so fast you can't even see those seconds make their little
streaks of re-entry into your heart.

Jan Kerouac, "Chapter 47"

From Cobblestone Gardens comes a pretty bird
Trapped in treacherous chicken wire, bird netting, and
flimsy fencing.

Debbie Dean, "Chicken Wire, Bird Netting & Flimsy Fencing"

Behind each eye here, one glowing weather.

Rumi

How graceful the small before danger!

Theodore Roethke, "Meditation At Oyster River"

Nothing move thee; nothing terrify thee; everything passes.

Saint Theresa of Avila

Figuring it all out no problem

giving it all up no problem

giving it all way no problem

devouring everything in sight no problem.

Diane di Prima, "No Problem Party Poem"

Playfully you hid from me.

All day I looked.

Then I discovered

I was you,

and the celebration of That began.

Lalla

the voices twisted losing all meaning

so I waited wondering how long until it was over.

or when it would start all over again.

Jolene G., "Chaos"

Which is worth more, a crowd of thousands,

or your own genuine solitude?

Freedom, or power over an entire nation?

Rumi

It's this simple

before I was with you now I'm here.

Hettie Jones, "Rabbits, Rabbits, Rabbits"

And I died a hero's death I sang in God's holy choir

I breathed a lonely dying breath I died a hero's death

Lizzy Lee Savage, "A Hero's Death"

Sing, my tongue; sing, my hand; sing, my feet, my knee,

my loins, my whole body.

Indeed I am His choir.

St. Thomas Aquinas

Every forest branch moves differently
in the breeze, but as they sway they connect at the roots.

Rumi

I cannot lose anything in this place of abundance I found.

St. Catherine of Siena

Madam, two hearts we brake,
And from them both did take
The best, one heart to make.

Michael Drayton, "The Heart"

What soul would bargain for a cure that brings
Contempt the nobler agony to kill?

George Meredith, "Modern Love"

The more love that it finds, the more it gives
itself; so that, as we grow clear and open,
the more complete the joy of heaven is.

Dante, "Italy"

Drawing on life of living clustered points
of light spun out of space.

Gary Snyder, "Song of the Taste"

AS I SEE IT, YES

I want to tell what the forests were like

I will have to speak

in a forgotten language.

W.S. Merwin, "Witness"

I came back to myself,

To the real work, to

"What is to be done."

Gary Snyder, "I Went Into the Maverick Bar"

And here I am, the center of all the beauty!

writing these poems!

Imagine!

Frank O'Hara, "Autobiographia Literaria"

I do not call it his sign,

I do not call it becoming one with his sign.

I do not call it union,

I do not call it harmony with union.

I do not say something has happened,

I do not say nothing has happened.

I will not name it You, I will not name it.

Now that the White Jasmine Lord is myself, what use for words at all?

Mahdeviyakka

Come spurre away

I have no patience for a longer stay,

But must go downe

And leave the chargeable noise of this great towne.

Thomas Randolph, "An Ode to Mr. Anthony Stafford to Hasten Him into the Country"

There is a desert I long to be walking,

a wide emptiness,

peace beyond any

understanding of it.

Rumi

O friends on this Path, my eyes are no longer my eyes.

A sweetness has entered through them,

has pierced through to my heart.

Mira

When I am Fifty shall my

face drift into those elongations

of innocence and confront me?

Frank O'Hara, "Poem"

The great sea has set me in motion,

set me adrift,

moving me like a weed in a river.

Uvavunuk, "Netsilik Eskimo"

Why should I share you? Why don't you get rid of someone
else for a change?

Frank O'Hara, "Meditations in an Emergency"

I am looking for a poem that says Everything so I don't have to
write anymore.

Tukuram

All things that love the sun are out of doors;
The sky rejoices in the morning's birth.

William Wordsworth, "Resolution and Independence"

Great expectation, wear a train of shame.

Sir Philip Sidney, "Astrophel and Stella"

Pain the soul, never mind the legs and arms!

Robert Browning, "Fra Lippo Lippi"

A sweet disorder in the dress
Kindles in clothes a wantonness

Robert Herrick, "Delight in Disorder"

The armies of the homeless and unfed;—
If these are yours, if this is what you are,
Then am I yours, and what you feel, I share.

Matthew Arnold, "To a Republican Friend"

I can't believe there's not another world where we will sit
and read new poems to each other.

Frank O'Hara, "To John Ashbery"

Out beyond ideas of wrongdoing and rightdoing,

there is a field. I'll meet you there.

Rumi, translated by John Moyne and Coleman Barks

WHATE'ER YOU DREAM, WITH
DOUBT POSSESSED,
KEEP, KEEP IT SNUG WITHIN YOUR BREAST.
ARTHUR HUGH CLOUGH, "ALL IS WELL"

I wish her store

Of worth may leave her poor.

Of wishes, and I wish—no more.

Richard Crashaw, "Wishes to His Supposed Mistress"

Mystical grammar of amorous glances;

Feeling of pulses, the physic of love;

Rhetorical courtings and musical dances;

Numbering of kisses arithmetic prove.

John Cleveland, "Marc Antony"

LOOK WITHIN

are you here? is he?

is she? she is. he is.

he is who?

ruth weiss, "Single Out"

Like a wind that sucks the sea,

Over and in and on the sea,

Good sooth it was a mad delight;

And every man of all the four

Shut his eyes and laugh'd outright.

William Bell Scott, "The Witch's Ballad"

Agonies are one of my changes of garments.

Walt Whitman, "Song of Myself"

Men are fools that wish to die!

Is't not fine to dance and sing

When the bells of death do ring?

Anonymous, "Hey Nonny No"

THESE HAVE THE SPIRIT'S RANGE,
THE MEASURE OF THE MIND:
OUT OF THE DAWN THE FIRE COMES FAST
TO CONQUER AND TO CHANGE.

C. DAY LEWIS, "IN ME TWO WORLDS"

Fie on sinful fantasy!
Fie on lust and luxury!
Lust is but a bloody fire,
Kindled with unchaste desire.

William Shakespeare, "The Merry Wives of Windsor"

Between living and dreaming there is a third thing.
Guess it.

Antonio Machado

YOU MAY RELY ON IT

Birth, old age,
Sickness, and death:
From the beginning,
This is the way
Things have always been.

Ly Ngoc Kiev

Some prisoned moon in steep cloud-fastness,—
Throned queen and thralled; some dying sun whose pyre
Blazed with momentous memorable fire;—
Who hath not yearned and fed his heart with these?

Dante Gabriel Rossetti, "The Soul's Sphere"

Tenants of the house,
Thoughts of a dry brain in a dry season.

T.S. Eliot, "Gerontion"

A wanderer is man from his birth.
He was born in a ship
On the breast of the river of Time.

Matthew Arnold, "The Future"

The luscious and impeccable fruit of life
Falls, it appears, of its own weight to earth.

Wallace Stevens, "Le Monocle de Mon Oncle"

He shall be strong to sanctify the poet's high vocation.

Elizabeth Barrett Browning, "Cowper's Grave"

Think of the language we two, same and not-same,
might have constructed from sign,
scratch, grimace, grunt, vowel:
Laughter our first noun, and our long verb, howl.

Maxine Kumin, "Nurture"

One instant is eternity; eternity is the now.
When you see through this one instant,
you see through the one who sees.

Wu-Men

HE WHO BINDS TO HIMSELF A JOY
DOES THE WINGED LIFE DESTROY.
BUT HE WHO KISSES THE JOY AS IT
FLIES LIVES IN ETERNITY'S SUN RISE.

WILLIAM BLAKE

There are moments when speech is but a mouth pressed
Lightly and humbly against the angel's hand.

James Merrill, "A Dedication"

TRY LOVE

I'll shed the tear of souls, the true

Sweat, Blake's intellectual dew,

Before I am resigned to slip

A dusty finger on my lip.

Stanley Kunitz, "Single Vision"

Without your intellectual and spiritual Values, man,
you are sunk.

James Merrill, "Charles on Fire"

Aye! be silent! Let them each hear each other breathing

For a moment, mouth to mouth!

Let them touch each other's hands, in a fresh wreathing

Of their tender human youth!

Elizabeth Barrett Browning, "The Cry of the Children"

O heart of stone, are you flesh, and caught

By that you swore to withstand?

Alfred Tennyson, "Maud: A Monodrama"

The little feet that patter here are metrical.

James Merrill, "From Up and Down"

I do not tell her, it would sound theatrical

Indeed this green room's mine, my very life.

We are each other's; there will be no wife;

The little feet that patter here are metrical.

James Merrill, "From Up and Down"

Pray but one prayer for me 'twixt thy closed lips,

Think but one thought of me up in the stars.

William Morris, "Summer Dawn"

I am fevered with the sunset, I am fretful with the bay.

Richard Hovey, "The Sea Gypsy"

In my travels I spent time with a great yogi.

Once he said to me,

"Become so still you hear the blood flowing

through your veins."

One night as I sat in quiet,

I seemed on the verge of entering a world inside so vast

I know it is the source of all of us.

Mira

My soul is full of whispered song,—
My blindness is my sight;
The shadows that I feared so long
Are full of life and flight.

Alice Cary, "Her Last Poem"

This is my dwelling, this is my truest home:
A house of clay best fits a guest of loam.

William Austin, "Verse 13: Sepulchrm Domus Mea Est"

Oh, they'll never let a man be good,
They whisper in his ear,
Until the fever heats his blood
To see the big ships clear.

Leo Hays, "Ports of Call"

Crescendo, and agape on the crumbling ridge
Stand in a row and learn.

W.S. Merwin, "The Drunk in the Furnace"

Be you all pleased? Your pleasures grieve not me.
Do you delight? I envy not your joy.
Have you content? Contentment with you be.

Lady Mary Wroth, "Sonnet IX"

SLEEP ON IT

This morning, timely rapt with holy fire,
I thought to form unto my zealous muse
What kind of creature I could most desire
To honour, serve and love, as poets use.

Ben Jonson, "Epigram LXXVI: On Lucy, Countess of Bedford"

Tell me, you anti-saints, why glass
With you is longer lived than brass?

Richard Corbett, "Upon Fairford Windows"

Yet have I been a lover by report,
Yea, I have died for love as others do.

Sir Robert Ayton, "Upon Love"

It is the echo of divine silence we hear the birds sing,
and that is the source of all we see and touch.

Tukaram

The spirit matters
Most of the words gone.

Joanna McClure, "Sappho"

I was sad one day and went for a walk;
I sat in a field.
A rabbit noticed my condition and came near.
It often does not take more than that to help at times—
to just be close
to creatures who
are so full of knowing,
so full of love
that they don't
chat,
they just gaze with
their marvelous understanding.

St. John of the Cross

Nature did her so much right
As she scorns the help of art.

William Browne of Tavistock, "Britannia's Pastorals"

Our hands imbibe like roots, so I place them on what is
beautiful in this world.

And I fold them in prayer, and they draw from the
heavens light.

St. Francis of Assisi

Then let us have our liberty again,

And challenge to yourselves no sovereignty:

You came not in the world without our pain;

Make that a bar against your cruelty.

Emilia Lanier, "Salve Deus Rex Judaeorum"

The spade, for labour stands.

The ball with wings

Intendeth flitting, rolling, wordly things.

George Wither, "The Spade"

Love built a stately house; where fortune came,

And spinning fancies, she was heard to say

That her fine cobwebs did support the frame.

George Herbert, "The World"

Spring overall. But inside us
There's another unity.

Rumi

I have no object to defend for all is of equal value to me.

St. Catherine of Siena

They dream only of America
To be lost among the thirteen million pillars of grass:
This honey is delicious
Though it burns the throat.

John Ashbery, "They Dream Only of America"

TAKE THE CHANCE

I am filled with you. Skin, blood, bone, brain, and soul.

Rumi

The Muses nine,

The nymphs divine,

Do all condole my woe.

George Chapman, "The Good Shepherd's Sorrow for the Death of His Beloved Son"

Being is not what it seems, nor non-being.

The world's existence is not in the world.

Rumi

Love made me poet, And this I writ;

My heart did do it, And not my wit.

Lady Elizabeth Tanfield, "Epitaph for Sir Lawrence Tanfield"

As in those thick clouds which the glove enclose
Th'all-working spirit were yet again to wade,
And heaven and Earth again were to be made.

Michael Drayton, "Noah's Flood"

That which creates a happy life
Is substance left, not gained by strife.

Mildmay Fane, Early of Westmorland, "A Happy Life"

I know how it will be when I die,
my beauty will be so extraordinary that God will worship me.

Rabia

I used to have fiery intensity, and a
flowing sweetness.
The waters were illusion.
The flames, made of snow.
Was I dreaming then?
Am I awake now?

Rumi

In vain, fair sorceress, thy eyes speak charms,
In vain thou mak'st loose circles with thy arms.

William Habington, "To a Wanton"

Self inside self,

You are nothing but me.

Self inside self,

I am only You.

What we are together will never die.

The why and how of this?

What does it matter?

Lalla

This poem is concerned with language on a very plain level.

Look at it talking to you. You look out a window

Or pretend to fidget. You have it but you don't have it.

You miss it, it misses you. You miss each other.

John Ashbery, "Paradoxes and Oxymorons"

Even I, while humble zeal

Makes fancy a sad truth incite,

Insensible away do steal;

And when I'm lost in death's cold night,

Who will remember, now I write?

William Harington, "Solum Mihi Superest Sepulchrum"

He thinks the moon is a small hole at the top of the sky,
proving the sky a quite useless for protection.
He trembles, but must investigate as high as he can climb.

Elizabeth Bishop, "The Man-Moth"

The furtive burrowing of birds singing in a frail
winter sun quiet singing quiet.

**Norbert Korte, "Throwing Firecrackers Out the Window
While the Ex-Husband Drives By"**

I will skip a lot of what happens next.
Then the moment comes.
Everything, everything has been said, and the wheels
start to turn.

Thomas Marvin Bell, "Ending with a Line from Lear"

I searched for my Self
until I grew weary,
but no one, I know now,
reaches the hidden knowledge
by means of effort.
Then, absorbed in "Thou art This,"
I found the place of Wine.
There all the jars are filled,
but no one is left to drink.

Lalleshwari

THE ANSWER LIES WITHIN

Why should we doubt, before we go

To find the knowledge which shalle ever last,

That we may there each other know?

Can future knowledge quite destroy the past?

Sir William Davenant, "Song, Endymon Porter and Olivia"

All day and night, music, a quiet, bright reedsong.

If it fades, we fade.

Rumi

And fools call Nature, didst hear, comprehend.

Accept the obligation laid on thee.

Robert Browning, "The Ring and the Book"

If God invited you to a party and said,

"Everyone in the ballroom tonight will be my special guest,"

How would you then treat them

when you arrived? Indeed, indeed!

Hafiz, "The Jeweled Dance Floor"

Why were you born when the snow was falling?

Christina Rossetti, "A Dirge"

You left North Haven, anchored in its rock,
afloat in mystic blue... And now—you've left
for good. You can't derange, or re-arrange,
your poems again, (But the Sparrows cab their sing.)
The words won't change again. Sad friend, you cannot change.

Elizabeth Bishop, "North Haven"

> # DIE WHILE YOU'RE ALIVE AND
> # BE ABSOLUTELY DEAD.
> # THEN DO WHATEVER YOU WANT:
> # IT'S ALL GOOD.
> ## BUNAN

Courage was mine, and I had mystery;
Wisdom was mine, and I had mastery

Wilfred Owen, "Strange Meeting"

I think God might be a little prejudiced.

For once He asked me to join Him on a walk

through this world, and we gazed into every heart on this earth,

and I noticed He lingered a bit longer

before any face that was weeping,

and before any eyes that were laughing.

And sometimes when we passed a soul in worship

God too would kneel down.

I have come to learn: God adores His creation.

St. Francis of Assisi

My peace is gone,
My heart is sore:
I'll find it never,
Ah, nevermore!

Johann Wolfgang von Goethe, "Faust"

> ## IF SOMETHING MY HEART CHERISHES IS TAKEN AWAY,
> ## I JUST SAY, "LORD, WHAT HAPPENED?"
> ## AND A HUNDRED MORE APPEAR.
>
> ### ST. CATHERINE OF SIENA

My Life had stood—a Loaded Gun
In Corners—till a Day
The Owner passed—identified
And carried Me away

Emily Dickinson, "My Life Had Stood—a Loaded Gun"

These hearts were woven of human joys and cares,

Washed marvellously with sorrow, swift to mirth.

The years had given them kindness.

Dawn was theirs,

And sunset, and the colours of the earth.

Rupert Brooke, "The Dead"

Where he stands, the Arch Fear in a visible form,

Yet the strong man must go.

Robert Browning, "Prospice"

The love of God, unutterable and perfect, flows into a pure
soul the way that

light rushes into a transparent object.

Dante

If I should break the chain, I felt my bird would go;

Yet I must break the chain, or seal the prisoner's woe.

Emily Bronte, "The Prisoner"

To learn the scriptures is easy,

to live them, hard.

The search for the Real

is no simple matter.

Deep in my looking,

the last words vanished.

Joyous and silent,

the waking that met me there.

Lalla

When the body becomes

Your mirror, how can it serve?

Mahadeviyakka

FOLLOW YOUR SAINT, FOLLOW WITH ACCENTS SWEET.

THOMAS CAMPIAN

Heartless she is as the shadow in the meadows
Flying to the hills on a blue and breezy noon.

George Meredith, "Love in the Valley"

There's no room for lack of trust, or trust.
Nothing in this existence but that existence.

Rumi

How have you left the ancient love
That bards of old enjoy'd in you!

William Blake, "To the Muses"

Fade far away, dissolve, and quite forget
What thou among the leaves has never known,
The weariness, the fever, and the fret
Here, where men sit and hear each other groan.

John Keats, "Ode to a Nightingale"

Alleluia! light
burst from your untouched
womb like a flower
on the farther side of death. The world-tree
is blossoming. Two
realms become one.

Hildegard of Bingen

Once my life is Your gesture, how can I pray?

Mahadeviyakka

If of herself she will not love,

Nothing can make her:

The devil take her.

Sir John Suckling, "Why So Pale and Wan?"

I give you my word

You pocket it

and keep the change.

Hettie Jones, "Words"

Who speaks the sound of an echo?

Who paints the image in a mirror?

Where are the spectacles in a dream?

Nowhere at all—that's the nature of mind!

Tree-Leaf Woman

Amid all forms visible, the spreading blades

I see as I move from place to place.

Osage, "The Song of the Maize"

God dissolved my mind–my separation.

I cannot describe now my intimacy with Him. How dependent
is your body's life on water and food and air?

Saint Theresa of Avila

SLEEP ON IT

8,000,000 alleluias

W.D. Snodgrass, "Snow Poems"

A little while alone in your room will prove more valuable than
anything else that could ever be given you.

Rumi

The hale and maimed together hurry to construct for the
Buddha a dwelling at each intersection.

Denise Levertov, "The Altars in the Street"

Rich the treasure;

Sweet the pleasure; Sweet is pleasure after pain.

John Dryden, "Alexander's Feast, or, the Power of Music"

And when the slope feels gentle to the point that climbing
up sheer rock is effortless as though you were gliding
downstream in a boat, then you will have arrived
where this path ends.

Dante

From the hag and hungry goblin That into rags would rend ye,
And the spirit that stands

By the naked man

In the book of moons defend ye

Giles Earle, "Tom o'Bedlam's Song"

Fair fools delight to be accounted nice. The richest corn dies if
it be not reaped; Beauty alone is lost, too warily kept.

Christopher Marlowe, "Hero and Leander"

Pause not to dream of the future before

us;

Pause not to week the wild cares that come o'er us

Frances S. Osgood, "Labor"

Change thy mind, since she doth change!
Let not fancy still abuse thee.

Robert Devereux, Earl of Essex, "Change Thy Mind"

When all my awareness is Yours, what can there be to know?

Mahadeviyakka

YOU CAN RELY ON IT

More of my days

I will not spend to gain an idiot's praise.

Thomas Randolph, "An Ode to Mr. Anthony Stafford to Hasten Him into the Country"

The sacred muse that first made love divine

Hath made him naked and without attire;

But I will clothe him with this pen of mine,

That all the world his fashion shall admire.

Sir John Davies, "Gulling Sonnets"

Ah, why did Fate his steps decoy

In stormy paths to roam,

Remote from all congenial joy?—

O take the Wanderer home!

James Beattie, "Retirement: An Ode"

The sky and the strong wind have moved the spirit
inside me till

I am carried away trembling with joy.

Uvavnuk "Netsilik Eskimo"

Quiet yourself. Reach out with your mind's skillful hand.

St. John of the Cross

Bind up the sagging breasts of morning
oh my darling let the light in.

Richard Shelton, "The Fourteenth Anniversary"

For how long did I stand in the house of this body
and stare at the road?

Mira

We were kings!—Now around us fall the shadows
Of our serfdom like a raven's dropping wings.
Not a footstep of a fairy in the meadows—
Not a comrade who remembers we were kings!

Will H. Oglivie, "Kings in Exile"

"Sit down and have a drink," he says.
I drink, we drink.

Frank O'Hara, "Why I Am Not a Painter"

Farewell, love, and all thy laws for ever,
Thy baited hooks shall tangle me no more.

Sir Thomas Wyatt, "A Renouncing of Love"

To see a World in a Grain of Sand
and a Heaven in a Wild Flower,
hold Infinity in the palm of your Hand
And Eternity in an hour.

William Blake, "Auguries of Innocence"

Ink runs from the corners of my mouth.
There is no happiness like mine.
I have been eating poetry.

Mark Strand, "Eating Poetry"

One star

Is better far

Than many precious stones.

Thomas Traherne, "The Apostarty"

The Truth has shared so much of Itself

With me

That I can no longer call myself

A man, a woman, an angel,

Or even pure

Soul.

Hafiz

I'll do as much for my true-love

As any young man may;

I'll sit and mourn all at her grave

For a twelvemonth and a day.

Anonymous, Traditional Ballad. "The Unquiet Grave"

I sing of apricot and brass.

Hidden coals glow sienna,

almost out of sight.

Pamela Crow, "Here"

Om

Shanti Shanti Om

The Buddha

What I know best is a little thing.

It sits on the far side of the simile,

The like that's like the like.

Charles Wright, "California Dreaming"

When to the sessions of sweet silent thought

I summon up remembrance of things past,

I sigh the lack of many a thing I sought.

William Shakespeare, "Sonnet XXX"

Draw, draw the closed curtains: and make room:

My dear, my dearest dust; I come, I come.

**Lady Catherine Dyer, "Epitaph on the Monument of
Sir William Dyer at Colmworth, 1641"**

Flowers bloom. Flowers die.

More is less.

I long for more.

Mark Strand, "The One Song"

I'd rather be a swineherd in the hut, understood

by swine, than be a poet misunderstood by men.

John Logan, "To a Young Poet Who Fled"

Before the leaves have formed

You can glimpse the Christ and Thieves on top of the hill.

One of them was saved.

That day the snow had seemed to drop like grace.

John Logan, "Spring of the Thief"

We moved in an hallucination born

Of silence, which like music gave us lotus

To eat, perfuming lips and our long eyelids.

Edith Sitwell, "Colonel Fantock"

I am severing all ties

With the parts of you

That swing from the rafters and

Hang from the trees.

perine parker, "marked up"

PROCEED WITH CARE

At this hour I am always happy,

ready to be taken myself, fully aware.

Lucien Stryk, "Awakening"

She lived in grace and beauty but never could she rid herself
the raven's guilty whisper.

Lizzy Lee Savage, "epitaph"

Move within, but don't move the way fear makes you move.

Rumi

No, fear not your wild thoughts
It is your mind that will keep you safe

ArtAmiss, "fortune"

Patience be all to thee.

Saint Theresa of Avila

"All wars are boyish," Herman Melville said;
But we are old, our fields are running wild:
Till Christ again turn wanderer and child.

Robert Lowell, "Christmas Eve Under Hooker's Statue"

Who will slap

my backside
When I am born
again.

Elise Cowen, "Who Will Slap…"

What is it you want to change?
Your hair, your face, your body? Why?
For God is in love with all those things and He might weep
when they are gone.

St. Catherine of Siena

In the fire of its making,
Gold doesn't vanish:
The fire brightens.

Mechtild of Magdeburg

MY PATH IS POINTED CONCEIVED OF REASONS UNKNOWN.

G. THOMAS, "UNTITLED"

If you circumambulated every holy shrine

in the world ten times,

it would not get you to heaven as quick

as controlling your anger.

Kabir

I don't feel that I have clarified enough or justified enough.

Jane Bowles, "Emmy Moore's Journal"

Bungee cords make perfect garters

Chromazona, "Sweet Cheeks"

we swallow

and clink together the last pieces of our

tinkertoy brains

perine parker "downtown"

Don't you want to be the gracious host

In a lovely home of which you're proud to boast?

When my girlfriends come to call

We've got to have carpeting from wall to wall.

Helen Adam, "Apartment on Twin Peaks"

Be the battle lost or won,

Though its smoke shall hide the sun,

I shall find my love—the one

Born for me!

Bret Harte, "What the Bullet Sang"

The poem

Is seen from all sides,

Everywhere,

At once.

Gary Snyder, "As for Poets"

REPLY HAZY

There was just a continent without much on it under a sky that never cared less.

William Stafford, "At The Bomb Testing Site"

I must not think of thee; and, tired yet strong,

I shun the love that lurks in all delight.

Alice Meynell, "Renouncement"

And tell those friends
About whom you forgot
That only half the word
Is *merde* and rot.

Madeline Gleason, "The Poet in the Wood"

His morning is not thine: yet must thou own
They have a cheerful warmth—those ashes on the stone.

Thomas Edward Brown, "Salve!"

Gather a shell from the strewn beach,
And listen at its lips; they sigh
The same desire and mystery,
The echo of the whole sea's speech.

Dante Gabriel Rossetti, "The Sea-Limits"

Friendship's face he loveth well:

'Tis a countenance whose spell
Sheds a balm o'er every mead and dell
Where we used to fret.

**Theodore Watts-Dunton, "Wassail Chorus at the
Mermaid Tavern"**

A box of counters and a red-vein'd stone,

A piece of glass abraded by the beach,

And six or seven shells,

A bottle with bluebells,

And two French copper coins, ranged there with careful art,

To comfort his sad heart.

Coventry Patmore, "The Toys"

I have left you behind

In the path of the past,

With the white breath of flowers,

With the best of God's hours,

I have left you at last.

Dora Sigerson, "Ireland"

Contrarious moods of men recoil away

And isolate pure spirits, and permit

A place to stand and love in for a day

Elizabeth Barrett Browning, "Sonnets from the Portuguese V"

For he saw what she did not see,

That—as kindled by its own fervency—

The verge shrivell'd inward smoulderingly.

Francis Thompson, "The Poppy"

Center of all centers, core of cores, almond self-enclosed and
growing sweet—all this universe, to the furthest stars and
beyond them, is your flesh, your fruit.

Rainer Maria Rilke

Eternal substance I do see,

With which enriched I would be;

What is invisible to thee.

Anne Bradstreet, "The Flesh and the Spirit"

Ye have robb'd,' said he, 'ye have slaughter'd and made an end,

Take your ill-got plunder, and bury the dead:

What will ye more of your guest and sometime friend?'

'Blood for our blood,' they said.

Henry Newbolt, "He Fell Among Thieves"

When there is no place

For the glow-worm to lie,

When there is no space

For receipt of a fly;

When the midge dares not venture

Lest herself fast she lay,

If Love come, he will enter

And will find out the way.

Anonymous, Seventeenth Century
"Love Will Find Out the Way"

The sodger frae the wars returns,

The sailor frae the main;

But I hae parted frae my love,

Never to meet again,

My dear—

Never to meet again.

Robert Burns, "The Farewell"

Life is but thought: so think I will

That Youth and I are housemates still.

Samuel Taylor Coleridge, "Youth and Age"

CONCENTRATE AND ASK AGAIN

I drove down an aisle of sound,
nothing real but in the bell,
past the town where I was born.

William Stafford, "Across Kansas"

Which way to heaven?
And where was love,
NEAR FAR NEVER
I forgot your name.

Madeline Gleason, "I Forgot Your Name"

Now air is hush'd, save where the weak-eyed bat
With short shrill shriek flits by on leathern wing.

William Collins, "Ode to Evening"

There is no living wind astir;
The bat's unholy wing
Threads through the noiseless olive trees,
Like some unquiet thing
Which playeth in the darkness, when
The leaves are whispering.

Nathaniel Hawthorne, "The Star of Calvary"

And time shall waste this apple-tree,

Oh, when its aged branches throw

Thin shadows on the ground below,

Shall fraud and force and iron will

Oppress the weak and helpless still?

Wiliam Cullen Bryant, "The Planting of the Apple-Tree"

veinless translucent against the

needle push the follicle folly

the cell collapse

perine parker, "cancer bath"

COULDST thou, Great Fairy, give to me

The instant's wish, that I might see

Harriet Prescott Spofford, "The Pines"

In a field

I am the absence of field.

Mark Strand, "Keeping Things Whole"

I've really had a mad year although now perhaps
I've come to a resting point...

Joan Burroughs, "Literary Outlaw"

And her proud, dark eyes wear a softened look

As she watches the dying embers fall:
Perhaps she dream of the knight in the book,
Perhaps of the pictures that smile on the wall.

William Gordon McCabe, "Dreaming in the Trenches"

Unwilling, alone we embark,
And the things we have seen and have known and
have heard of, fail us.

Robert Bridges, "On a Dead Child"

And each victor, passing wanly,
Gazes on that Presence lonely,
With unmoving eyes where only
Grow the dreams for which men die.

Madison Julius Cawein, "Attainment"

Of all things beautiful and good,
The kingliest is brotherhood.

Edwin Markham, "Brotherhood"

PERHAPS

She too accepts the truth, there is no way back.

Denise Levertov, "Stele"

These things in which we have seen ourselves and spoken?

Ask us, prophet, how we shall call

Our natures forth when that live tongue is all

Dispelled, that glass obscured or broken.

Richard Wilbur, "Advice to a Prophet"

O, well for him that knows and early know

In his own soul the rose

Secretly burgeons, of this earthly flower

The heavenly paramour.

Alfred Noyes, "The Two Worlds"

I know that no flower, no flint was in vain

on the path I trod.

Amelia Josephine Burr, "A Song of Living"

When brother shall with brother walk in peace,

Watching the kindly fruits of earth increase;

And all the energies beneath the dome

Shall find the harmony that roots in Home.

Richard Burton, "The Plan"

I would make a list against the evil days
Of lovely things to hold in memory.

Richard Le Gallienne, "A Ballade-Catalogue of Lovely Things"

What riches have you that deem me poor,
Or what large comfort that you call me sad?

George Santayana, "What Riches Have You"

He didn't know much music
When first he come along;
An' al the birds went wonderin'
Why he didn't sing a song?

Frank Lebby Stanton, "The Mocking-Bird"

O you that still have rain and sun,
Kisses of children and of wife,
And the good earth to tread upon,
And the mere sweetness of life,
Forget not us, who gave all these
For something dearer, and for you.

Laurence Binyon, "From the Dead to the Living"

Love thy country, wish it well,

Not with too intense a care;

'Tis enough that, when it fell,

Thou its ruin didst not share.

George Bubb Dodington, Lord Melcombe, "Shorten Sail"

Be as I content With my old lament

And my idle dream.

Robert Bridges, "Clear and Gentle Stream"

Lord, in this hour of tumult,

Lord, in this night of fears,

Keep open, oh, keep open

My eyes, my ears.

Hermann Hagedorn, "Prayer During Battle"

Now rain, now sun, now clouds that jackknife in between.

Rod McKuen, "Hand in Hand"

a bee buzzed through my open window following the breeze

and the quiet order of things.

Jolene G., "Chaos"

Oh, what is so good as the urge of it,

And what is so glad as the surge of it,

And what is so strong as the summons deep,

Rousing the torpid soul from sleep?

Angela Morgan, "Work"

COMRADES, POUR THE WINE TONIGHT
FOR PARTING IS WITH DAWN!
RICHARD HOVEY, "COMRADES"

Yet no blind fears distress the thoughtful soul.

David Fallon, "Nature's Miracle"

Faithful paranoid

It's all One to you isn't it

Real, that is.

Elise Cowen, "Death"

It is good to be out on the road, and going one knows
not where.

John Masefield, "Teweksbury Road"

He whom a dream hath possessed treads the
implacable marches.

Shaemas O'Sheel, "He Whom a Dream Hath Possessed"

God mend thine every flaw,

Confirm thy soul in self-control,

Thy liberty thy law!

Katharine Lee Bates, "America the Beautiful"

ANYTHING IS POSSIBLE

It matters not how strait the gate,

How charged with punishments the scroll,

I am the master of my fate:

I am the captain of my soul.

William Ernest Henley, "Invictus"

You come upon it suddenly—you cannot seek it out:

It's like a secret still unheard and never noised about.

Charles Hannon Towne, "The Best Road of All"

folklore extremis is a

deadly disease only

cured by offering water

Brenda Knight, "speed poem, part 1"

The river that flows

Over the rock

Hesitates

At the dam

Dolores G., "A Higher-ku"

I will laugh with the wicked

I will cry with the heathens

and I will dance for my dead.

Bucky Sinister, "Shine"

Let me live in a house by the side of the road

Where the race of men go by—

The men who are good and the men who are bad,

As good and bad as I.

Sam Walter Foss, "The House by the Side of the Road"

Reader, by now you must be sure you know
just where we are, deep in symbolic woods.

Irony, self-accusation, someone else's suffering.
The search is that of art.

William Matthews, "The Search Party"

I know they boast they souls to souls convey:

Howe'er they meet, the body is the way.

William Cartwright, "No Platonique Love"

Meditate within eternity.

Don't stay in the mind.

Your thoughts are like a child fretting

near its mother's breast, restless

and afraid, who with a little guidance,

can find the path of courage.

Lalla

Shall I go bound and you go free,

And love one so removed from me?

Padraic Colum, "Shall I Go Bound and You Go Free?"

Still through the cloven skies they come,
With peaceful wings unfurled;
And still their heavenly music floats O'er all the weary world

Edmund Hamilton Sears, "The Angels' Song"

From too much love of living,

From hope and fear set free,

We thank with brief thanksgiving

Whatever gods may be.

Algernon Charles Swinburne, "The Garden of Prosperine"

Are you jealous of the ocean's generosity?

Why would you refuse to give this joy to anyone?

Fish don't hold the sacred liquid in cups.

They swim the huge fluid freedom.

Rumi

All that we see or seem

Is but a truth within a dream.

Edgar Allan Poe, "A Dream Within a Dream"

Life is given.

Nothing is earned,

so learn to serve others,

not your own desire and greed

and ego. They steel your energies,

whereas devotion builds your strength

and protects the intelligent flame

that leads to the truth within.

Lalla

CHOOSE TO LIVE LIFE

I walk slow through day break-blue.

back to north beach.

my lids fold around my whole being.

ruth weiss, "I Always Thought You Black"

O where are you going? stay with me here!

Were the vows you swore me deceiving?

No, I promised to love you, dear,

But I must be leaving.

W.H. Auden, "O What Is that Sound"

If you want money more than anything,
you'll be bought and sold.

If you have a greed for food, you'll be a loaf of bread.

This is a subtle truth: whatever you love, you are.

Rumi

He who, from zone to zone,

Guides through the boundless sky thy certain flight,

In the long way that I must tread alone,

Will lead my steps aright.

William Cullen Bryant, "To a Waterfowl"

There is no snow in Hollywood there is no rain in California

I have been to lots of parties and acted perfectly disgraceful
but I never actually collapsed.

Frank O'Hara, "Poem"

He who replies with words of Doubt Doth
put the light of knowledge out.

William Blake, "Auguries of Innocence"

In the heats of hate and lust
In the house of flesh are strong,
Let me mind the house of dust
Where my sojourn shall be long.

A.E. Houseman, "From a Shropshire Lad"

How funny you are today New York like
Ginger Rogers in Swingtime.

Frank O'Hara, "Steps"

Since moons decay and suns decline
How else should I end this life of mine?

John Masefield, "The Passing Strange"

Did I go mad in my mother's womb
Waiting to get out.

Elise Cowen, "Did I Go Mad"

Are you jealous of the ocean's generosity?
Why would you refuse to give this joy to anyone?
Fish don't hold the sacred liquid in cups.
They swim the huge fluid freedom.

Rumi

Her pleasure will not let me stay.

She talks and I am fain to list.

Robert Lee Frost, "My November Guest"

They're cheering from the ferries,

And they're waving from the shore;

The dull old life's behind us

And the new life lies before.

Anonymous, "Sailing Orders"

When will my shame fall away?

When will I accept being mocked

and let my robe of dignity burn up?

Lalla

> # DON'T GET OLD AND MEAN AND BITTER,–
> # THERE'S A PRIMAL REMEDY–
> # JUST TAKE A SHIP TO SEA, MY LAD,
> # JUST TAKE A SHIP TO SEA.
> ## HARRY KEMP, "THE REMEDY"

The weight of arrogance is such that

no bird can fly

carrying it.

St. John of the Cross

Infinity is here dig it.

Norbert Korte, "Turning 40 in Willits"

Complaint is only possible while living in the suburbs of God.

Hafiz

We shall remember, when our hair is white,

These clouded days revealed in radiant light.

**George Orwell, "Our Minds Are Married,
But We Are Too Young"**

I do not doubt I am limitless, and that the
universes are limitless,

in vain I try to think how limitless

Walt Whitman, "Assurances"

THE FATES ARE AGAINST IT

It is your destiny to see as God sees,

to know as God knows,

to feel as God feels.

Meister Eckhart, "Germany"

I had a natural passion for fine clothes, excellent food, and

lively conversation about all matters that concern

the heart still alive. And even a passion

about my own looks.

Vanities: they do not exist.

Saint Theresa of Avila, "Spain"

And henceforth I will go celebrate anything I see or am,

And sing and laugh, and deny nothing.

Walt Whitman, "All Is Truth"

Lay down these words

Before your mind like rocks.

placed solid, by hands.

Gary Snyder, "Riprap"

I have had to learn the simplest things

last. Which made for difficulties,

Even at sea I was slow, to get the hand out, or to cross

A wet deck.

The sea was not, finally, my trade.

Charles Olson, "Maximus, to Himself"

It's the old shell trick with a twist:

I saw God put Himself in one of your pockets.

You are bound to find Him.

Tukaram

I wish for such a lot of things

That never will come true,

And yet I want them all so much

I think they might, don't you?

Sara Teasdale, "Wishes"

It is always a matter, my darling,

Of life or death, as I had forgotten. I wish

What I wished you before, but harder.

Richard Wilbur, "The Writer"

My friend at last comes back.

Maybe the right words were there all along.

Complicity. Wonder.

C.K. Williams, "The Gas Station"

He openly declared that it was the best sign

Of good store of wit to have good store of coin.

Sir John Suckling, "A Session of the Poets"

More time, more time. Barrages of applause

Come muffled from a buried radio.

The New-year bells are wrangling with the snow.

Richard Wilbur, "Year's End"

O well for him whose will is strong!

He suffers, but he will not suffer long;

He suffers, but he cannot suffer wrong.

Alfred Lord Tennyson, "Will"

The thing you're after

May lie around the bend.

Charles Olson, "I, Maximus of Gloucester, to You"

Someone's road home from work this once was,

Who may be just ahead of you on foot

Robert Frost, "Directive"

I cannot dance, o Lord, unless You lead me.

Mechtild of Magdeburg

O how feeble is man's power,
That if good fortune fall,
Cannot add another hour
Nor a lost hour recall.

John Donne, "Song"

Love in her eyes sits playing,
And sheds delicious death.

John Gay, "Love in Her Eyes Sits Playing"

What I most want
is to spring out of this personality, then to sit
apart from that leaping.
I've lived too long where I can be reached.

Rumi

If sadly thinking
With spirits sinking,
Could more than drinking
My cares compose.

John Philpot Curran, "The Deserter"

Give all to love;
Obey thy heart.

Ralph Waldo Emerson, "Give All to Love"

He wrote with no apparent hesitation, quickly, and with
concentration; his inspiration was inspiring.

C.K. Williams, "The Critic"

Love is form, and cannot be without
important substance (the weight
say, 58 carats each one of us, perforce
our goldsmith's scale).

Charles Olson, "I, Maximus of Gloucester, to You"

Some day the viewless latch will lift,
The door of air swing wide.

Henry Augustin Beers, "Ecce in Deserto"

God is a pure no-thing, concealed

in now and here:

the less you reach for him, the more

he will appear.

Angelus Silesius

Say not the struggle nought availeth,

The labour and the wounds are vain,

The enemy faints not, nor faileth,

And as things have been things remain.

Arthur Hugh Clough, "Say not the Struggle nought Availeth"

Love, you have wrecked my body. Keep doing that.

I am more well with this deep ache of missing you than

content with the physical wonders you can pacify us with.

Mira

Three silences there are: the first of speech,

The second of desire, the third of thought

John Greenleaf Whittier, "The Three Silences of Molinos"

ASK AGAIN LATER

I wonder when the tide will flow,
Sir Oracle cease saying, "No"

John Davidson, "Rondeau"

Some day the viewless latch will lift,
The door of air swing wide.

Henry Augustin Beers, "Ecce in Deserto"

A little while for scheming
Love's unperfected schemes;
A little time for golden dreams

Philip Bourke Marston, "After Summer"

Therefore I send you my poems that you behold in them
what you wanted.

Walt Whitman, "To Foreign Lands"

O clear intelligence, force beyond all measure!
O fate of man, working both good and evil!

Sophocles

Pretentious giving me

What in the instant

I knew better of

Charles Olson, "The Librarian"

Dear God, please reveal to us your sublime beauty that is everywhere, everywhere, everywhere, so that we will never again feel frightened.

My divine love, my love, please let us touch your face.

St. Francis of Assisi

Build as though wilt, unspoiled by praise or blame,

Build as thou wilt, and as thy light is given.

Thomas Bailey Aldrich, "Enamored Architect of Airy Rhyme"

I ask all blessings, I ask them with reverence,

of my mother earth, of the sky, moon, and sun my father.

I am old age: the essence of life, I am the source of all happiness.

All is peaceful, all in beauty, all in harmony, all in joy.

Anonymous. "Navajo"

Leave the sick hearts that honor could not move

Rupert Brooke, "Peace"

Order is a lovely thing;
On disarray it lays its wing,
Teaching simplicity to sing.

Anna Hempstead Branch, "The Monk in the Kitchen"

I drag a boat over the ocean
with a solid rope.
Will God hear?
Will he take me all the way?

Lal Ded

God was an accident of language,
a quirk of the unconscious mind, but
Unhappily never of my mind.

C.K. Williams, "The Ladder"

You will die, no doubt, but
Die while living.

Edgar Lee Masters, "Edmund Pollard"

The Mind severe and cool;
The Heart still half a fool;
The fine-spun Soul, a beam of sun can startle.

Elinor Wylie, "This Corruptible"

Tread near the living, consecrated thing,

Treasure me thy cast youth.

Francis Thompson, "Before Her Portrait in Youth"

With your bucket of water, and mop, and brush,

Bringing her out of the grime.

Thomas Hardy, "The Statue of Liberty"

THE REPLY IS YES

These two have striven half the day,

And each prefers his separate claim,—

Poor rivals in a losing game,

That will not yield each other way.

Alfred Lord Tennyson, "In Memoriam A. H. H."

You tell too many lies and hurt your-self:

You don't like what you only like too much.

Robert Browning, "Fra Lippo Lippi"

What canst thou say or do of charm enough

To dull the nice remembrance of my home?

John Keats, "Lamia"

ACKNOWLEDGMENTS

To all the billies, the beats, the seers, the saints

The poets, the pagans, and the pirates

To our ever-loving and deadline-forgiving publisher and friend

To the Leos, the Steampunks, the stars

To the Pisces husband and the lifelong lovers and friends

We thank you

You know who you are

And you know how to find us

Write us a speed poem about it.

BIBLIOGRAPHY

Aldington, Richard. *The Viking Book of Poetry of the English Speaking World*, Vol. 1. Viking Press: 1958, New York.

Alvarez, Alicia. Bedtime: *365 Nightly Readings for Passion and Romance*. Conari Press: 1995, Berkeley.

Astrov, Margot. *American Indian Prose and Poetry*. Capricorn Books: 1962, New York

Benet, William and Conrad Aiken. *An Anthology of Famous English and American Poetry*. The Modern Library/Random House: 1945, New York.

Bloom, Harold. *The Best Poems of the English Language*. Harper Collins: 2004. New York, New York.

Brown, E.K. *Victorian Poetry*. Thomas Nelson and Sons: 1942, New York.

Burr, David Stanford. *Love Poems*. Barnes & Noble: 2002, New York, New York.

Cooper, Alice Cecilia. *Poems of Today*. Ginn and Company: 1924, Boston.

Dickinson, Emily. *Selected Poems*. Dover: 1990, New York.

Douglas, George. *The Book of Scottish Poetry*. T. Fisher Unwin: 1911, London.

Eliot, G.R. and Norman Foerster. *English Poetry of the Nineteenth Century*. Macmillan: 1935, New York.

Fowler, Alastair. *The New Oxford Book of Seventeenth Century Verse*. Oxford University Press: 1992, Oxford/ New York.

Frothingham, Robert. *Songs of the Sea & Sailors' Chanteys.* Houghton Mifflin: 1924, Cambridge, MA.

Goodwin, Daisy. *101 Poems That Could Save Your Life.* Harper Collins: 2003, New York, New York.

Harmon, William. *The Top 500 Poems.* Columbia University Press: 1992, New York, New York.

Hebel, J. William and Hoyt H. Hudson. *Poetry of the English Renaissance 1509-1660.* Appleton-Century Crofts: 1929, New York.

Hyde, Douglas. *Love Songs of Connacht.* Barnes & Noble: 1969, New York.

Kaufman, Alan. *The Outlaw Bible of American Poetry.* Thunder's Mouth Press: 1999, New York.

Keats, John. *Lyric Poems.* Dover: 1991,New York,.

Lattimore, Richmond. *Greek Lyrics.* The University of Chicago Press: 1960, Chicago.

Martz, Louis Lohr, Ed. An*chor Anthology of Seventeenth-Century Verse* Volume 1, and 2. Anchor Books: 1969, Garden City, New York

McKuen, Rod. *Hand in Hand.* Pocket Books: 1977. New York, NY

Nicholson, D.H.S. and Lee A.H.E. *The Oxford Book of English Mystical Verse.* Clarendon Press, Oxford: 1917

Plath, Sylvia. *Ariel: The Restored Edition.* Harper Collins: 2004, New York.

Quiller-Couch, Arthur Thomas, Sir. *The Oxford Book of Ballads.* Clarendon Press, Oxford: 1910.

Quiller-Couch, Arthur Thomas, Sir. *The Oxford Book of English Verse.* Clarendon Press: Oxford, 1901.

Rittenhouse, Jessie Belle. *The Little Book of Modern Verse.* Houghton Mifflin: Boston, 1917.

Rossetti, Christina. *Goblin Market and Other Poems.* Dover: 1994, New York.

Sewell, Marilyn. *Claiming the Spirit Within.* Beacon Press: 1996, Boston.

Shakespeare, William. *Measure for Measure.* New American Library: 1964, New York

Sinister, Bucky. *All Blacked Out and Nowhere to Go.* Gorsky Press: 2007, Los Angeles.

Smith, Phillip, Ed. 100 *Best-Loved Poems.* Dover Books: 1995, Mineola, New York.

Tedlock, Dennis. *Finding the Center: Narrative Poetry of the Zuni Indians.* The Dial Press: 1972. New York

Whicher, George F. *The Goliard Poets.* Cambridge University Press: 1944, Cambridge, MA.

Zeydel, Edwin. *Vagabond Verse.* Wayne State University Press: 1966, Detroit.

The following link proved tremendously useful for finding sources for poetry: www.bartleby.com

ABOUT THE AUTHOR

Cerridwen Greenleaf has worked with many of the leading lights of the spirituality world including Starhawk, Z Budapest, John Michael Greer, Christopher Penczak, Raymond Buckland, Luisah Teish, and many more. She gives herbal, crystal and candle magic workshops throughout North America. Greenleaf's graduate work in medieval studies has given her deep knowledge she utilizes in her work, making her work unique in the field. A bestselling author, her books include *Moon Spell Magic, The Book of Kitchen Witchery, The Magic of Gems and Crystals* and the *Witch's Spell Book* series. She lives in the San Francisco Bay Area.

Mango Publishing, established in 2014, publishes an eclectic list of books by diverse authors — both new and established voices — on topics ranging from business, personal growth, women's empowerment, LGBTQ studies, health, and spirituality to history, popular culture, time management, decluttering, lifestyle, mental wellness, aging, and sustainable living. We were recently named 2019's #1 fastest growing independent publisher by *Publishers Weekly*. Our success is driven by our main goal, which is to publish high quality books that will entertain readers as well as make a positive difference in their lives.

Our readers are our most important resource; we value your input, suggestions, and ideas. We'd love to hear from you — after all, we are publishing books for you!

Please stay in touch with us and follow us at:

Facebook: Mango Publishing
Twitter: @MangoPublishing
Instagram: @MangoPublishing
LinkedIn: Mango Publishing
Pinterest: Mango Publishing

Sign up for our newsletter at www.mango.bz and receive a free book!

Join us on Mango's journey to reinvent publishing, one book at a time.